MY HAUNTED REALITY

BY RICK WAGNER

MY HAUNTED REALITY

Library of Congress
Cataloging in Publication Data

Wagner, Rick
My Haunted Reality

1st edition, August 2017

Printed in the United States of America

ISBN: 978-1-54963-246-4

CONTENTS

INTRODUCTION

Do you ever get a feeling that you are not alone and that there is something more to life as we see it? There are spirits around us all the time leaving us messages. If only we would just take the time to notice them.

Why are they here?

What are they trying to tell us?

What is the difference between a ghost and a spirit?

Do they have any influence on us?

I have answers to these and so many more questions from a lifetime of experiences and encounters. I survived a Near Death Experience (NDE) on a motorcycle that changed my whole perspective of life and afterlife. I have developed a new understanding and perception of the unexplained things happening around us.

Our fear of ghosts has been instilled in us because of what Hollywood has put into our heads. We need to see past all the horror movies and recognize that spirits do have a reason for being here. My stories increasingly revealed a reality to me that I had rejected at first because I did not understand what I was being shown. It was like spirits were testing me to see how I would respond. The more they allowed me to see, the more the fear dissipated and I could begin to accept and appreciate all that I was witnessing.

As I began performing energy clearings for my clients, I was always aware of feeling more than just the energy in the room. This sensitivity developed into an empathetic form of communication with the spirits around my clients allowing me to receive information about them and their reasons for being here. I truly appreciate my ghosts and I wouldn't be alive right now without them!

Growing up, I would see things that terrified me and wondered why no one else saw or felt what I was experiencing. As a young boy, it was hard for me to comprehend that there might be a reason for ghosts to be here. I'd be lying in my bed, frozen with fear, unable to defend myself thinking that ghosts were going to drag me out of my bed or at least eat my toes. It wasn't until after my near death experience that I understood more of what was going on. They are not trying to scare or hurt us, but are just trying to get our attention.

Some spirits just want us to know they are nearby and are trying to help and comfort us, while others have a message that they need to share. They may want to tell a loved one that they are happy and doing fine where they are, or maybe a need to settle an unresolved issue or concern with someone. Other times they can be hopelessly lost and in need of a little help and guidance. Whatever their reason, this close proximity to humans can end up unintentionally causing us great pain and anxiety.

I can tell my stories now without fear, but these aren't just stories. Everything here actually happened. It took me a long time to come to terms with the overwhelming cascade of emotions, thoughts, and feelings I was experiencing. Once I realized these spirits have a purpose for being here, I started sharing my stories and helping people understand the energies and spirits around them. Almost everyone I talk to has a ghost story of their own that they share openly with me. For others, I explain that closing your eyes does not make them go away.

Even with our eyes wide open, it is very easy to ignore all of the warning signs around us. For example, when I was riding my motorcycle, people would always warn me about the inevitable accident looming ahead. "If you ride a bike, it's not IF you are ever going to have an accident, but WHEN!" they would tell me. I listened but never paid much attention. I still loved riding my bike everywhere until that fatal day had arrived. It wasn't until I survived my near death experience on the motorcycle that I realized how much our lives can be guided and protected by the spirits around us.

I also received other warnings as I was doing one of my favorite activities, renovating old houses. These places would inevitably be haunted and as I formed my own bond with my ghosts, I was warned on several occasions to stop going in the direction I was heading in. "You don't know what you're getting into!" some people would tell me. They'd say, "You're going down a very dangerous road. Not all ghosts are going to be your friend!"

I didn't understand what all the warnings were about. No one ever told me what they might do. It's not like you ever see on the news, "Ghost Bludgeoned Homeowner with Knife!" They don't seem to have those capabilities. They do seem to have messages for us, but what happens on the day when you open a door to the spirit world that you cannot close and finally discover what all the warnings were about? I had the opportunity to experience that for myself and that was the day my life almost ended.

During the time I was renovating homes, most of my encounters were ghosts of children. They seemed to be content where they were, consistently doing things in my houses that only kids would do. I actually enjoyed their company, but sometimes their behavior went overboard. On those occasions, I would yell at them during the night, "Ok, now! Instead of turning the television on and off all night, how about washing the windows and floors? Let's try putting all that energy into good use!" .. To no avail.

Even when I was preparing to sell my favorite haunted property, my real estate agents advised not telling anyone about my affinity with the ghosts in the house. There may be some people who would find that information disturbing, but I found that hard to believe. Really? I love my ghosts. How could this information not be an asset? It's like having 24/7 security that does not have to rely on electricity to work or monthly payments to keep the service active. The spirit services are free and are included in the purchase price!

I began to learn why they were here and what effects they were having on us. Many times spirits get lost or stuck and can't find their way back to where they are expected to be. I have also observed in cases where death was sudden and unforeseen, the spirit hasn't had time to process what just happened to them and therefore they don't realize they are dead yet. The old remedy was always to direct spirits to "go into the light". Which light are they referring to? There are far too many lights in the spirit world to just randomly send them into a light. It's confusing for them.

Through my exploration, I discovered an ability to direct them back to where their family and loved ones are waiting for them. This love connection through their family and relationships creates a stronger bond and ultimately, the happiest place for them to be. Most spirits are happy and relieved to discover a lost family member or loved one. The others, I would just let them stay in the house and live with me, as long as they don't break anything or scare the neighbors.

There is a dangerous side to all this and if I wasn't on such good terms with my own spirit guides, it could have cost me my life. What I eventually experienced was a frightening understanding of how and why the extremely lost ones are able to influence us with feelings of hopelessness, isolation, despair, and even thoughts of suicide. I've never felt these emotions before and I was extremely fortunate to have found a way to alleviate them.

These energies actually do have substantial meaning and effects on our lives and having the proper information and knowledge develops our understanding and sensitivity of the spirits and energies around us. Learning as much as we can about our existence here and being able to answer some of the rudimentary questions of life is a great way to increase our awareness. It is wonderful to see the door of possibility and acceptance opening up more and more as we continue to explore a world of spirituality, unexplained phenomena and what I like to call, "My Haunted Reality".

TESTIMONIALS

Completing an apology.

"When I first met Rick we were sitting and chatting at a restaurant bar in LA. Rick mentioned that there was a woman who was standing next to me but when I turned to look, there was no one there. He said that the woman is someone I should know and was very close to. She wants to apologize for something she had done and was resting her hand on my right shoulder. I told Rick I've been having pain in that shoulder for over a year now. He described my mother, who had recently passed away. She took me out of her will because she did not approve of the man I was seeing. We have since then split up and I'm sure my mother is now feeling very guilty about her actions.

Rick explained to my mother that when spirits touch us, it gives us pain because they are connecting to our electrical centers including the spine, neck, shoulders or head. We let her know that her actions regarding the will were forgiven and the moment she stepped back, the pain in my shoulder was gone. I felt such a relief knowing that this chapter in my life was over and both my mother and I could move on. Thank you, Rick, for providing me the information and guidance I needed."

Deborah, CA

A message of love.

"My father had passed away about 4 months before I saw Rick at the gym. He said he wanted to walk with me to the parking lot and had something he needed to tell me. Rick had never met my father and knew nothing about him. "Your father was a big man, wasn't he?" he asked. I told him that he was and asked him how he knew that. Rick said, "He had big hands. While I was working out, I felt his hand on my shoulder. I could feel the warmth and the emotion from this man pouring down on me. It was like sitting under a waterfall of love, emotion, and information. He wants you to know how much he loves you and how proud he is of you and everything you are doing now."

Rick said he found it hard to find the words to describe the sheer amount of love, affection and pride my dad had for me. I was very emotional myself after hearing this and have always been grateful and supportive of Rick and the messages he receives. He was able to reconnect me to my dad in a very special way that I will never forget."

Boris Schaak, CA

No exorcisms allowed.

"I was not the only person who felt something strange every time I entered my apartment. I had just ended a long relationship and wanted Rick to clear out the old energy and do an exorcism on my place. Rick told me that he does not do exorcisms and does not want to just "get rid of entities". That only makes them angry and then they get mad at him. He explained he could have a conversation with whatever was there and see how he can help. He not only regenerated my space by clearing out the old energy but was able to re-connect me with my grandmother, Agnes, who was not an evil entity at all. I am very grateful and comforted to know she is still around and I was very impressed with what Rick was able to do."

Ken, CA

No longer lost.

"I had Rick come over and do a clearing on my home, and I was also dealing with a bad neck and shoulder pain. Rick was able to see a male spirit with his hand on my shoulder. He then reconnected this spirit with his daughter on the other side and my pain

11

that I had been experiencing for over 2 years, was gone. An hour later a most wonderful and amazing thing happened. My heart filled up with an abundance of love and happiness. It was the spirit letting me know he was no longer lost. He was with his daughter now and where he was supposed to be. It was so profound and lovely to be a part of such an experience. The ecstatic feeling of joy and happiness lasted for several hours. Bless you, Rick and thank you."

Cynthia Harris, CA

Understanding death.

"Rick has a unique gift of connecting the spirit world with the human world. I was very confused about the fear and anxiety I was having after the recent death of my sister and then my mother. He gave me a greater understanding of a dynamic connection that only I could know, relate to and understand. He is now showing me how to hold on to an awareness of them in the present and how to keep them close in my thoughts and in my heart."

Constance B., CA

A ghost or a spirit.

"I moved into a new apartment and was not able to sleep. I felt something heavy in my space and whatever this was, it wanted a lot of attention. It would wake me up in the middle of the night by shaking my bed and there was no one else in the room. Rick explained the difference between a ghost and a spirit as a ghost is just a spirit that somehow got stuck. He was very in tune with this spirit and reconnected him with a family member on the other side. I am finally able to have a relaxed, full night of much-needed sleep."

John Maldonado, FL

Disruptive energies.

"Rick has an amazingly intuitive and insightful connection with the spirit world around us. He has the ability to communicate and redirect spirits that are lost and explains what happens when we come in contact with them. I can see how his understanding of this world could benefit others by offering clarity and peace from these sometimes disturbing and disruptive energies."

Denise Lynn, NYC

No more pain.

"Working with Rick is a magical experience! I hired him for a client who had unusual electrical and plumbing failures constantly in his home. In addition, my client was suffering from severe back pain after multiple surgeries. These upsets continued happening over the past 10 years in the house that he shared with his partner. I could feel there was an interfering, denser energy but did not know what was happening or why.

After an hour with Rick, I could feel the shift in the house and its energy. Immediately following the redirection of the spirit, my client could feel his shoulders and legs release. Each day after the work with Rick, my client sent me texts with more and more healing and energy shifting! It was truly a profound healing experience for my client and the spirits involved.

I would strongly recommend Rick for anyone with unexplained occurrences, pain, injuries or depression."

Kristen Bomas, FL
Speaker/Author/Seminar Leader

Cloud lifting

"For several years I had been experiencing some unexplained, negative energies around me which were impacting me physically, mentally, and emotionally. When strange electrical issues arose with my car that could not be resolved, I couldn't ignore the situation any longer. Rick came highly recommended and from the first conversation, I could feel a change in the energy around me. Rick put was able to put into words exactly what I was feeling, which was intriguing to me as I was never able to define what I was going through myself. I immediately noticed an increase in my energy. There were obvious changes in my health and mood and I was once again able to connect and interact with the people around me. I had this great feeling of clarity as if a cloud was lifted from around me."

Jarrod, FL

Spirit Connection.

"For several months I suffered from dark thoughts, depression, and a constant nagging that I just wasn't myself. I tried botanicas, home cleansings, positive affirmations, and read almost every book on ghosts and possessions I could get my hands on, but there was no one I could talk to until I was referred to Rick. Upon our first conversation, he immediately sensed a presence around me, confirming my suspicions. Rick has first-hand experience with spirit attachments and reminded me that spirits of the dead can affect the living, but not to be feared, as they are in as much pain as those they inflict it upon. He was not only concerned about my well being but knew that love and empathy for the lost spirit were essential as it needed attention and reunion with a loved one to move on, which he helped it do. After only one phone session, I felt more at peace, balanced, and grounded with a new outlook on life with a purpose.

Thank you, Rick, for reinforcing the belief that life is more than meets the eye, life is about the journey of our souls."

Tim P.

Paranormal Investigator

TYPICAL EMAILS I RECEIVE

"I don't understand what happened to me. I was always happy and content with my life, but for the last six months I've been getting deeply depressed, body aches and strange feelings in my house, even thoughts of suicide. I know this is not me but feels like something has connected to me and is talking me into this state every day. Can you please clear this away from me so I can get my life back? I haven't told anyone about this, not even my wife and kids. Thank you!"

"There is something in my space giving me great anxiety and heart palpitations. I lost my abusive husband to suicide some time ago and need to make sure he's not back causing me more pain."

"Rick, there are so many strange things happening in my life right now. I'm feeling very lethargic, depressed, and invisible to others. Even my car is failing now. Can you help me?"

"I really need your help. Not for me, but for my daughter. Every time she spends a night with me, she is frightened by a spirit in my house. This spirit is touching her and holding her down. Please! Please! I need to know who it is and what message they are trying to give her!"

"I have been renovating and selling homes in Florida that have been foreclosed and the energies in these homes are dark and depressing. Can you please clear them for me so people will be able to move into a clean and happy new home? Also, the home I'm selling now has a spirit in it that needs to be relocated. Thank you for your help!"

"Hi, Rick! I am looking forward to working with you. This neck/shoulder pain just won't go away. I've had it for some time now and been to chiropractors, acupuncture, massage therapy and even the x-rays have shown nothing. There's also a disturbing energy in my house that needs to leave."

"My home has some sort of dark energy interference problem in it. I will contact you tomorrow to set up a time to schedule a clearing/extraction. Thank you again!"

"I moved into this new apartment with my boyfriend and every night the kitchen appliances are turning on by themselves. This is freaking us out. Can you help?"

"Rick, there have been some changes in my living situation and I need you to come out clear whatever it is out of my home. The energy here is uncomfortable and disturbing, which makes it hard to sleep! I need your help again."

"I work out of my home and lately it's been hard to concentrate on my design work. I feel like my business is slipping away and the stress now is overwhelming. I can't seem to find a way out and I'm feeling incredibly stuck. Can you come clear this stuff out so I can be doing what I'm supposed to be doing?"

"I'm forwarding you a client of mine that needs help with an entity in his home. I do hypnotherapy work, but this is something more than hypnosis can cure and seems to be right up your alley, Rick. Good luck!"

"I didn't want to bother you over the weekend, but I started to get this weird electrical energy running up and down my spine and legs. The intensity is increasing and I feel like I'm that movie, "The

Conjuring". I can also feel the floor underneath me shake. There is something in the new house that is sucking all the energy out of it.

I need you to come over and help me with all of these issues. Thank you!"

Chapter 1

MY MOTORCYCLE REALITY

I have always been a huge fan of motorcycles. What an amazing way to engage and become one with the world around you. The road has your full attention. You aren't texting, talking on the phone, changing a radio station or playlist, eating or fixing your hair. You can feel the road beneath you, the wind pressing against your body and experience the smells and sounds of each city and countryside as you pass through. Riding always gave me a feeling that the world was unfolding before me for my eyes only. My own personal panorama. That right now, right here at this moment I was the only person on the planet viewing this incredible scene before me.

My first time on a bike was while I was in college at Syracuse University. My best friend, Bill Clisson, had a small 250cc Honda and taught me how to ride. I fell in love with it and actually ended up buying the bike from him. A few months later he took off on a road trip with a girlfriend on a pair of larger 400cc motorcycles. They planned on crossing the country and ending up in California.

That sounded amazing to me. What an adventure. I had a bike now and soon I would also have friends who lived in California! I'm sure mom and dad weren't thrilled with the idea of me leaving college to drive out to Los Angeles on a motorcycle, but they supported me as they always had in the past. Aerospace Engineering wasn't holding my attention anymore, so I packed up my things, told my Engineering professors goodbye and drove home to Buffalo to prepare for my big trip.

Once I was home, I bought a duffle bag for my clothes, a sleeping bag and a backpack for everything else, including my Rand McNally Road Atlas. This was a large road atlas that showed every road from New York State to California. This was 1975 and there was no GPS back then and no cell phones. If I was riding and approached an intersection where I wasn't sure which road I should take, I would have to pull over, stop and get off the bike. I'd take off my helmet, open my backpack and pull out the atlas, locate the state I was in, and find the exact street and intersection I was standing on and determine the correct road I needed to proceed. Then I'd have to pack it all up again, put on the helmet, get back on the bike and go.

Before I left, I remember taking a picture of my mom sitting on my bike with my dad standing behind her, his hands placed gently on her shoulders. Mom looked a little worried, but mom was always the great worrier in the family and I wondered how she was able to remain so calm about my new adventure.

We were raised in a wonderfully cozy 3-bedroom house in Buffalo, New York. Besides me, there was my mom and dad, my brother, two sisters, and the added pleasure of having my grandmother live with us as well. I just loved having so many people around who loved and supported each other. My grandmother had passed away two years earlier and for the first time in my life, I had to deal with the loss of someone very close to me. Our family had this strong empathetic connection, so I always felt very connected to grandma, even after her death.

I had no idea how long the trip would take and never took the time to consider all of the things that could possibly happen along the way. I had too many close calls including getting squeezed between two enormous transport trucks whose tires would be at the same height as my head while passing in opposite directions and just inches from my handlebars. I just

23

closed my eyes at that point and assumed I was already a goner! Once I opened my eyes and realized that the oncoming truck had passed by me and I was still alive, I could then safely pull in front of the truck I was attempting to pass. Another advantage of having a really small bike.

I would be caught rounding precarious turns while being distracted by the magnificent vistas and just barely being able to pull the front wheel back onto the road before I would have ended up soaring over a cliff and crashing into a ravine. I was mugged in Washington, D.C., had a flat tire in the middle of nowhere down South and even rode my bike straight into the same path a hurricane had created after blowing away most of Pensacola, Florida. Each time something happened that made my heart feel like it was going to explode inside my chest, I would have this amazing reassurance that someone was helping me not kill myself. I was not alone. I had this comforting feeling that my grandmother was not going to let anything happen to me and that I'd make it to California in one piece.

People along my route would notice that this little motorcycle had a New York State license plate on it and could not believe how far I had driven. They'd ask me where I was headed and I would yell back, "California!" After that, everyone always seemed compelled to share some horrible story about someone they knew, or a neighbor or relative who was in a tragic motorcycle accident and which limb they lost. I'd try to smile and let them know how much I appreciated them sharing their touching story with me and I assured them I would be extra careful while driving. "Remember, it's not IF you are going to have an accident, but WHEN!" they would yell. Thank you. I really didn't need to hear that. Were they trying to warn me of something inevitable or were all of these messages just a concerned reminder for my safety?

So, this little bike of mine had a very small engine. I could get amazing gas mileage and average around 200 mpg, but pushing the bike over 60 mph created a lot of vibration. My trip started in August while the weather was still warm. I didn't realize I'd still be on the road through September and into October when the nights started to get very cold. I learned a trick to stay warm from a fellow rider. I'd buy a newspaper and use it to line my jean jacket for insulation. This worked great unless it was raining. Sometimes at night, I would have to pull over when I found a welcoming roadside diner because the vibration of the bike and the cold was making me shake uncontrollably. I'd try to warm up with a cup of hot soup, but it was as if I was having periodic seizures that would send chills through my body. My soup would never make it to my mouth and end up spilling all over me. The poor waitress would come over to see if I was ok and I'd tell her that the soup was just so good that my body was over-reacting to the exquisite flavor!

Without any form of musical stimulation, especially on those long stretches of highway, I would sing to help keep myself awake. It always sounded great inside my helmet and would help keep my brain occupied. Occasionally, I would forget I was still singing and be caught belting out a song at a stoplight. I'd turn and suddenly realize I was not alone. I'd see people staring at me from their car window wondering what I was doing. I'd pretend I was coughing or that I had just swallowed a bug.

After surviving the endless straight roads of Texas and detouring to the Grand Canyon and Las Vegas, I finally made it to Los Angeles in one piece. Thanks, Grandma! I was able to locate my friends and together we made memories of even more road trips to Palm Springs, Angela's Crest Highway and up the coast of California. I didn't stop there. I wanted to see Europe. I flew to Paris and then Nice where I rented a motorcycle. I toured the south of France from Nice to the palace in Monte Carlo and down to Cannes and St. Tropez.

I remember leaving St. Tropez too late because it was already getting dark and I only had a pair of sunglasses to protect my eyes. I opted for the faster road back to Nice, not along the coast, but on the Autoroute. I found myself maneuvering up and down hills with winding roads while cars were flying by me at 120 mph. I had no helmet on my head for protection and could barely see the dimly lit road ahead of me through the dark sunglasses. After arriving safely back in Nice, I realized just how very lucky and grateful I was to have once again avoided the possibility of a fatal disaster.

I owned a car, but my motorcycle was still my favorite choice of transportation. I remember driving home at night after work and panicking as I found myself surrounded and penned in by large delivery trucks. I've been chased by crazed drivers taking out their road rage on me because I could drive between the cars and they couldn't. I had lots of close calls, but always felt fortunate that I was saved each time. I always made it home ok. No fateful accident. Maybe all those warnings about a motorcycle accident were meant for someone else. They probably were unaware that I had an invisible grandmother watching over me!

There was a time when you could legally ride your motorcycle without a helmet strapped onto your head. That sounds so crazy now, but I would ride my bike to the gym all the time and never wore a helmet! One afternoon in June, I was packing up my gym bag. This was not your normal gym bag. Someone had given me a Mandarina Duck bag a while ago and I used it for my gym clothes. This was like a messenger bag with a shoulder strap. The bag itself was wrapped with these cool looking foam ribs, more for design than function. I threw some clothes and a towel into the bag, pulled on a tank top, my gym shorts, then my socks and sneakers. This was 1990 and those baggy EG Smith socks were still very popular poking out above your high top sneakers. I stuck my head through the strap on my bag and headed out the door.

I started up the bike and headed west down Sunset Boulevard for my short ride to the gym. I no longer had the small Honda motorcycle, but upgraded to a nice 400cc Honda Shadow which was a much smoother ride. The new bike was not as good on gas as my little bike, but this one was much faster, heavier and so much more powerful.

Some days, I would get to the gym early and just lie out by the pool for a few minutes to relax, usually waking up half an hour later filled with guilt because I fell asleep when I should have been working out. On this particular day, I opened my eyes and saw nothing but blue sky and a few scattered clouds. As I was waking up, I remember I was heading to the gym and I assumed I decided to hit the pool instead. I must have really needed this nap since I still felt so groggy and was having a hard time waking up. Today felt a little different for some reason. As I watched a few birds fly overhead, I could hear the sound of an approaching vehicle, getting louder until I saw the tire of a car pass within inches of my head!

This was not a dream and there are no cars that would pass that close to the pool. I lifted my head to see my body splayed in the middle of the road. I noticed that my motorcycle seemed awfully far away and about an equal distance behind me was the green Jaguar that must have hit me. Well, I need to get up and see what happened to my bike.

I could move my head around without any difficulty, but when I tried to sit up, my body was unresponsive. I felt like a turtle with my head poking out of a shell. My head and neck seemed to be ok, but the rest of my body was just lying there and I couldn't move. I tried to focus on specific body parts to generate a response. My fingers were not cooperating, so I thought I'd try my arm. "Ok, right arm! Up! Come on, let's GO! One! Two! Three! Up!" but no response. Then, I tried the other arm, "Left arm! Let's go!" I really wanted to get up before someone sees me here. I kept thinking of how embarrassing it would be if someone I knew was to drive by and see me laying in the middle of the street like this! It is a fascinating experience to review your thoughts in a time of crisis. I just wanted desperately to get up off the street and back on my bike.

Just then a little red Mercedes coupe pulls up, the window rolls down and a pleasant looking man asks me if he should call 911. I said that might be a good idea since I'm not able to move anything. My head was resting nicely on my foam-ribbed Duck gym bag and I have no idea how long I was lying there. As the driver of the red Mercedes made the phone call on one of those big black early model car phones, he wished me luck and pulled away. I nodded and yelled a thank you for his help.

There was no one else around now and it was quiet. I turned my head to the left and glanced over at the green Jag and I could see a woman still sitting in the car. Maybe she was injured and couldn't get out. I had no idea how bad the accident was. I'm just lying in the street staring at the sky and contemplating my unresponsive body. Looking in the other direction, I

30

could see my poor motorcycle. It was several driveways away, laying on its side with twisted handlebars on the opposite side of the road. I was wondering how it managed to get so far away from me and if I'd be able to straighten it out enough to drive it home.

The next thing I remember was the sound of an ambulance. I could see the red flashing lights approaching and I began to worry when I saw how fast it was gaining on me. What if the driver didn't see me in the street and he was thinking I was over by the car? I can't wave him down and he wouldn't hear me yell over the siren. I wouldn't be able to get out of the way. Thankfully, the emergency vehicle slowed down, made a u-turn and backed up to me while two men jumped out with blue suits on. One of the paramedics knelt down next to me and asked if I had any pain. "No", I said. "Nothing hurts, but I can't feel anything. I can't move anything either." Wow, I thought. I'm lucky to be feeling no pain right now. Then there was that terrifying thought that slowly started to sink into my brain. If I can't feel my legs, how would I know if they are still working? What about my arms? My hands? If I can't feel anything, I also can't tell if anything is broken, severed or ruptured. After being so active my whole life, I can't imagine what it would be like not to have full control and use of my body.

He asked me where my home was. I said I live a few blocks away. These guys were professionals and I think he could sense I was starting to realize my situation and what the after effects of this accident might be. To prevent me from going into a worst-case scenario, or even a state of shock, the paramedic offered to cheer me up by asking me another question.

"Well, do you know what the blonde did when she found out that most accidents happen within a mile of your home?"

"Um, no. What did she do?" I said.

He replied, "She moved!"

Ok. That made me laugh. It was nice to realize that I could laugh! I saw my chest moving up and down and knew that my lungs and heart must be working ok. I'm still breathing.

Then he asked me who put the gym bag under my head. Since I wasn't able to move, I wasn't repositioning myself on top of my bag hoping for a more comfortable position. I told him, "My grandmother did." When he asked me where she was, I told him, "She died 10 years ago."

Once he asked the question, I had an instant replay of the event in my head. I was able to see myself letting go of the motorcycle and flying through the air. Along my right side, I could see my grandmother's face and hands as she took the gym bag from behind my back and moved it in front of me. As I was about to collide with the pavement head first, my head landed on my gym bag. There was nothing to protect my body from the impact of the pavement, outside of my gym shorts and t-shirt. The blow resulted in the paralysis and lack of feeling in my extremities that I was now dealing with.

The paramedics lifted a gurney off the ambulance and lowered it to my level. I was swiftly and carefully picked up and placed onto a stretcher and lifted up to the gurney. They then wheeled me into the back of the ambulance. This created an interesting point of view. After seeing so many hospital shows on TV, we are always looking down at the person that has just been brought in. Now I'm seeing everything from a new perspective. I'm looking up.

From the blue sky to the white metal top of the vehicle to the variations of afternoon sunlight as we drove down a very nice residential street lined with beautiful trees. I could see the trees flying past, which was wonderful to see, but now I was distracted by our very loud siren. I was wondering if we really needed all that noise? What if I get a headache, can I feel it?

I'm fine. In fact, slow down. I don't want you to have an accident on the way to the hospital. Plus, your driving is making me nauseous. I'm not used to viewing the world from this angle.

After so many jarring stops and speeding up and fast turns, we arrived at the hospital. The doors flew open while a team of white jackets pulled me from the vehicle. I sprout wheels and the dizzying ride continued through sliding glass doors and into extremely bright lights. We flew through another set of doors, into a small room and then … the questions.

"What day is today?"

"Do you know today's date?"

"Where were you heading?"

"Are you aware of what just happened?"

"What is your name?"

"What were you driving?"

"Hey!" I said. His last question made me realize I had left something behind! I asked, "Who is going to take care of my motorcycle? We just left it there in the street and someone might take it! The keys are still in it!"

The paramedic assured me the bike was damaged past the point of anyone trying to ride it again. All this was happening so fast. Shouldn't I tell someone where I am? Oh. Ok. So I can't use my fingers to dial anyone and remember this was before we all had cell phones stuck to our bodies.

Now they seem intent on taking my clothes off and finally someone walks up to the bed I'm lying on with information for me. The new doctor said, "We're going to have to run a series of tests to see what kind of internal injuries we are dealing with and also find out more about the paralysis." I was hoping they weren't thinking of putting me into one of those metal tubes for CAT scans or MRI's. I get claustrophobic and might have a panic attack!

I was not given any pain medication or even aspirin in case there were any internal injuries that needed to be addressed. If something ruptured and I couldn't feel it, how would I know it ruptured? They also did not want me to fall asleep. By the time they were beginning my tests, I was starting to feel a tingling sensation in my fingertips. I was hoping this was a good sign.

Then the tests started. For the MRI and CAT scan machines, I had to close my eyes and pretend that I was lying on a beach somewhere. The clanging of the MRI helped keep me awake. After all the tests were done, I was taken to another room. My feet and hands were tingling like they had fallen asleep and I could move my torso from side to side. All this seemed encouraging.

They kept me awake all night and by the next morning, I was exceptionally tired. I remember seeing my friend, Tony, standing at the foot of my bed. One of the doctors had called him, told him where I was and what had happened. There were three other ER doctors standing to my right with clipboards to deliver the results of the tests.

The head doctor said, "First of all, this was a very bad accident. Both the car and the motorcycle were totaled. You are very lucky to be alive. The paramedics told us how far you traveled from the initial impact to where they found you on the pavement. You should have at least fractured your skull or severed your spine, but both were fine. We also have the results of the CAT scan and MRI, which showed no internal injuries. The other issue that we all found fascinating was that for landing on pavement with no protective gear, there were no open wounds. No blood. The paralysis was temporary from the impact and everything seems to be returning to normal. We have no reason to keep you here, but if you experience any pain at all later, please let us know as soon as possible. So with that, you are officially discharged and free to go."

I walked out of the hospital feeling very grateful, but confused. The full reality of what happened took several days to sink into my brain. So Grandma saved me again. Did the paramedic respond when I told him that she put my bag under my head? He had no idea at the time that I would be totally fine and walk out of the hospital the next day on my own. I started to appreciate my life more and experience gratitude on a whole new level. I had a wonderful feeling wash over me that everything was going to fine.

I don't want to say I felt like I was indestructible and nothing could hurt me. I'm still human, but I had just experienced something miraculous and along with that, so many more questions began to surface. That was a very dramatic way to show me that it was not my time to go. Why not take me now? That would have been a great opportunity for me to move on. Maybe there is a lesson I still need to learn, or something I need to do that would serve a greater purpose.

The motorcycle accident was a big transition for me. Up until this point, every time I saw or felt something around me, it terrified me. It made me realize that there had to be a better reason for spirits to be here than to scare us. If my grandmother was one of those spirits, then obviously they weren't here to terrify us. Maybe these forces, energies, and entities are around us to help us and guide us. This was just the beginning of my education of ghosts and spirits and each step of the way lead to a better understanding of why they are here.

My journey begins when I was just six years old back in Buffalo, NY where I first started seeing things...

Chapter 2

GROWING UP SCARED

1961

I had an interesting assumption growing up in Buffalo, New York. I thought that the entire world received the same amount of snow that we did during one of our normal winters. Why would it be different any place else? The world was covered with snow and everybody gets to go outside and play in it. We'd build castles, forts, snowmen, and have snowball fights. Behind our house was a hill that led up to the railroad tracks. We were never supposed to go near the tracks but were allowed to use the hill to go sledding on our toboggans, sleds, flying saucers and even in cardboard boxes if nothing else was available. Anytime we found ice, we could ice skate, play hockey or just slide around knocking each other down.

As we got older we were attracted to some of the much bigger hills just southeast of Buffalo, where we would learn to ski! This skiing consisted of ski classes taught on a hillside of mostly solid ice where the instructor would constantly check our faces for frostbite when the temperatures were below zero. We were extremely motivated to ski down the hill as fast as possible so we could go indoors in hopes of feeling our fingers, noses, and ears again. How much fun was that! I guess as long as we kept moving, we wouldn't freeze to death. What a great world to grow up in. Afterward, we always had this wonderfully warm house to run home to, pull off all our frozen outerwear and go thaw out.

I had a favorite place for thawing. Mom always sat in the same place on the couch, closest to the TV. I'd jump onto the couch, cover up with a nice blanket and slide my frozen feet under her nice warm thighs. As I would let out an audible sigh of relief, she'd yell at me, "Stop that! Your feet are like ice!" I'd tell her that I almost had frost bite out there and there's no other way for me to get the circulation back into my feet. The things mothers endure for their children.

My family lived in a small 3-bedroom house filled with 7 people and only 1 bathroom. Mornings and nights meant having to wait in line to go to the bathroom and brush your teeth. When there wasn't enough room to play in the living room, we had a basement that was the perfect place to escape. During the summer it was nice and cool, and in the winter it was warmer than going outside when it was freezing. We'd all play down there often during the day.

I never liked going down there at night. There were only three bare light bulbs in the ceiling and they all had different switches. At the top of the stairs was a light switch for the bulb at the bottom of the stairs. The other two were on opposite sides of the basement, back by the furnace and each had a metal chain you had to pull to turn them on. In the meantime, shadows were already forming on the walls, around the furnace, and under the stairs and it just wasn't a comfortable feeling.

I was still the youngest, so I wasn't allowed to watch horror movies or anything too scary because it might give me nightmares. The only difference was in my house it wasn't the movies I was scared of, but my older brother, Bill, my older sister, Judy, and even my dad. My family loved hiding in closets and behind doors and under tables or wherever they could just so they could scare me. Even if I knew there was no one upstairs, I'd still have to open the door quickly and jump inside just in case someone was hiding so I'd get to scare them first. When in doubt, always be the aggressor.

That wasn't even the worst of it. My mom and dad slept in the downstairs bedroom before my youngest sister Meg was born. There were 2 small bedrooms upstairs. The smaller one I shared with my brother Bill and across the hall, my sister Judy was sharing with my grandmother. I think I was around 6 or 7 years old when I began waking up in the middle of the night because I sensed someone else was in the room with us.

I would slowly open up my eyes thinking someone was standing over me and wanting to talk. I could feel a heaviness in the room that would make it almost hard to breathe. Every hair would stand on end from my toes to the top of my head, but I kept my eyes closed so I wouldn't have to see anything. I'd bend my legs up under me so it wouldn't be able to bite my toes if they were sticking out of the bottom of the blanket. If I kept my eyes closed, it would go away, right?

I would usually just fall back asleep knowing that my brother is just inches away and he'd protect me if anything was trying to get me. Also, I had Grandma and Judy right there in the next room. By the time morning came and I was still alive, I would have forgotten about whatever it was that was down there by the foot of the bed. It never came out during the day so I could run around the house freely.

This went on for quite some time and I don't think I ever told anyone, probably because it never killed me if that's what its intention was. The appearances were infrequent but the feelings were getting stronger. Instead of hiding inside the wall at the far end of the bedroom, it seemed like it was getting closer to the foot of the bed each night. I found that if I closed my eyes tight and pulled the blankets over my head, that seemed to help make him go away and I'd fall back asleep. Each morning I would check to make sure I still had all my toes.

One night when I was finding it hard to breathe, I woke up and actually looked down at the bottom of the bed. I saw the same white figure as always, crouching down against the wall. This time I could see him moving like he was preparing to jump. It was a warm night so both bedroom doors were wide open and I couldn't believe no one else in the house knew what was happening here. There's something in our room trying to get us, or at least, me, and no one is coming to help? What is wrong with you people?

I need to alert the house, so I'll just scream as loud as I can for Grandma, then she will wake up and see him. I don't know why I thought I needed to get to my grandmother when my brother was so nearby. I opened my mouth to scream and nothing came out. I could breathe, but my voice was gone. I tried again harder and still no sound. I was trying to think how he could control my voice and stop me from screaming. Maybe he thought if I was screaming I wouldn't be listening to anything he might be trying to tell me.

I wanted to get out of bed and run but knew he would catch me, so I just laid there waiting for him to jump. I wouldn't move at all, pretending to be asleep so when he finally jumped on me, I'd be prepared to do something. I was not at all sure what, but I was

43

ready. If he did jump on top of me, I could always roll to my side and throw him on top of my brother. Bill was bigger and older than I was and he'd know what to do with this white ghost. Then I could run and get help. Bill would be able to handle him ok unless he had one of his asthma attacks. I'll just have to make sure his asthma spray is still sitting at the top of the bed. I don't know if he'd be able to fight off a ghost and use his asthma inhaler at the same time. He usually has a slight coughing fit after inhaling the stuff. At least I had a plan now. I would be the aggressor!

Hiding back under the covers again, I fell asleep. In the morning, I'd push back the covers and in the light of day, everything had returned to our old, safe bedroom once again. No longer filled with dark shadows and white crouching ghosts. Since no one else had any idea that all this going on, I didn't want them to think I was crazy and I didn't want anyone else to be scared, so I wouldn't mention it. Plus, I still had all my toes and none of them were chewed off.

His appearances became less and less and eventually, he stopped showing up at night. I often wondered what happened to him. Perhaps he went off to terrify some of the neighbor's kids in the area and chew on their toes. Sometime later Mom had pulled out one of our many old photo albums and we started looking at pictures. After flipping through a few pages, my heart stopped. There was a picture held in place with those little black corner photo holders of a man with white hair and white pajamas sitting on a twin bed. When I pointed to the picture and asked who that was, my mother said that was her father. He had bad rheumatoid arthritis and was bedridden for almost 30 years. He was not able to walk. This was the exact image of my crouching white ghost!

That is how I always saw him. That is why he was crouching down on the floor against the wall. Here I was thinking he was about to jump on me. He manifested as he had lived, possibly thinking I'd recognize him as he had lived for the last 30 years. He died in 1952 at only 61 years of age and before I was born so I never met him, at least not while he was alive. I had never even seen his photo until that day we started looking through the old album. Here was the ghost that terrified me for so long. My own grandfather!

I felt terrible that this man had made so many attempts to communicate with me and I only shut my eyes and pulled the blankets over my head wishing he would go away. I wonder if I just wasn't so scared, maybe I could have understood the wonderful message he was trying to get to her. Now I can see why I was reaching out so desperately to my grandmother. Her husband was only trying to tell her that he was ok. I was too overwhelmed with fear to realize that had been his purpose.

I hope he can forgive me.

Chapter 3

INDIAN BURIAL LAND

1981

I look back now and recall the terror I experienced and wonder if that could be the reason why no other ghosts decided to try and contact me again. Maybe they didn't want me to die prematurely of a heart attack from too many contacts with ghosts, even if the ghosts were family! I still had encounters but felt that they were just trying to get my attention to make sure I didn't forget they were still around me, watching me.

I remember in 1981 my best friends at the time rented a house out on Fire Island for the summer. They invited me to come and stay, but they'd only be able to be there on weekends. They worked in New York City during the week as did the other 8 million people living in Manhattan back then. I'd have to fend for myself during the week, or at least until they arrived on Saturday. That would be fine with me. I'm sure I'd find something to keep myself busy. This was back in a time before cell phones and there was no television reception on the Island. I was not aware of the lack of entertainment until I actually arrived.

From Manhattan, you hop onto the Long Island Railroad toward Sayville, change trains in Babylon, grab a shuttle to the dock where a ferry boat would take you out to the Island. There are no roads on the Island, only raised wooden plank walkways. Any groceries, bags or luggage had better come with wheels or you would be carrying them for quite a distance. The Pines grocery store has these cute little red wagons that you could borrow when available. This is why any construction or repair work involving demolition is so difficult. There is truck access, but it is very limited. You would have to carry or drag your things down a long wooden plank walk that would eventually lead to your house.

This house was off the main walkway on the bay side of the island. It was quieter here and more secluded. There were no streetlights and the island was covered with trees. You must have a flashlight or you could easily end up falling off the wooden walkway. The house was a 2-story structure with 2 bedrooms and 2 bathrooms. From the walkway, there was a bridge entering into the 2nd floor and the living room. This floor also had a kitchen, small bathroom, and a dining room that lead to a large outdoor deck. Downstairs were the 2 bedrooms and another bathroom accessible by a steep spiral metal stairway, very dangerous when in a hurry and wearing socks.

I unpacked and took a few minutes to get acquainted with my new surroundings. After a few days of swimming, running up and down the beach, shopping and going to bed early, I started looking around for something more to do. There were no laptop computers available then and the few books I found in the house weren't very interesting. Then, over on the bottom of a shelf in the living room, I found a puzzle! It was a great big box with hundreds of pieces of trees that all looked the same. It might take forever to finish, but I thought it would be fun putting this huge puzzle together before my friends arrived here at the house on Saturday. That way I can show them how productive I was all week. I'd work on it for a bit in the morning before hitting the beach and then again at night after dinner. By Friday night I thought I'd have it compete.

It was a picture of a beautiful landscape covered with trees and hundreds of green leafy puzzle pieces. After many hours, working after dinner through the dim lighting, I remember pressing the last few pieces into the puzzle. I was feeling very proud of myself for having completed such an enormous task. The full size of the completed puzzle was about 3 feet by 4 feet and must have had at least 2 million pieces, or least it seemed to have that many. I took a deep breath and stood back to admire the work I had done. As I looked at the puzzle again, there, right in the center, was a gaping hole! A space screaming at me that I was not done yet. I still need one more piece to complete the puzzle.

I looked on the table and inside the box, but could not find it. I started checking under the table, on the floor and even under the refrigerator, inside all the drawers and cabinets and still nothing. I was thinking, "You can't do this to me! All that time working on the puzzle and you're going to keep ONE PIECE from me finishing this masterpiece? That's torture!" I continued looking and even thought of checking downstairs, but it was too dark now. I'll look around in the morning when I have more light. I climbed into bed that night feeling frustrated. The perfectionist in me was not happy at all. I'll just have to try to forget about it for now and worry about it in the morning.

Saturday morning was beautiful and bright. My first thought was how easy it was going to be to find that pesky puzzle piece. I got dressed and started planning on what needed to be before their arrival here this afternoon. I'd have plenty of time to go to the gym and grocery store in the little downtown area by the dock. There was only one grocery store, so if they were sold out of whatever you were looking for, you were out of luck. That was it. No other options.

I walked up the cold, metal spiral staircase to the even brighter living room light and opened the doors to let in some fresh air. As I walked into the kitchen to make some breakfast, I stopped cold. The hair on my arms and neck began to stand up as I glanced down at the puzzle. Remembering all my thoughts of frustration for not having completed what I started, I was now staring down at a fully completed puzzle. There was no more gaping hole, no more empty spaces yelling at me. I leaned over the puzzle and tried to remember which one was the one that was missing and tried to come up with a reasonable explanation of how it got here. The pieces all looked the same. The missing one was deeply colored with black and dark green leaves and there were already so many of them. I ran my hand over the top of the puzzle, feeling for any variations or bumps that might give me a clue as to how this had happened. I felt nothing. It was all smooth, just as it was supposed to be.

I never came back upstairs last night. All the doors were locked and no one else was in the house. That's when your brain starts thinking of other crazy possibilities. No one else knew I was even working on a puzzle or that a piece was missing. I never felt there was anything else in the house, since my arrival. If there was a ghost in the house, it was probably a friendly one because now I didn't have to spend my entire morning looking for a piece of puzzle.

I thanked my phantom puzzle-helper, finished my breakfast and headed to the gym. I stopped by the grocery store and bought some things for lunch and dinner for all of us and then headed back to the house. When I unlocked the door and walked inside, the first thing I looked at was the puzzle. I thought to myself if that piece is gone again, I'm probably going to freak out and start screaming. No need to scream. The piece was still there just as it was when I left. I unpacked the groceries, made myself a sandwich for lunch, then cleaned up the kitchen and headed downstairs to take a shower. As I was singing in the shower, I was noticing again how quiet it was. All I hear is birds, and that was nothing to complain about. I just hoped the birds weren't complaining about my singing.

I was starting to get a little sleepy and my friends weren't arriving for a few hours yet. I don't know why, but the bed in the master bedroom was looking mighty comfortable and if I just laid down on it for a short nap, I'm sure they wouldn't mind. I kicked off my shoes and climbed on top of the big fluffy down comforter. As soon as my head hit the pillow, I was out.

I have no idea how long I slept, but it was a very deep sleep. What woke me was the sound of footsteps approaching on the walkway above. Are they here already? I should get up and straighten the bed, but it was so amazingly comfortable I just didn't want to move. So, I decided to just stay put.

I heard the footsteps continued over the bridge to the door. This sounded like only one set of footsteps. I wonder why one of them was coming out alone? I hope they didn't have another fight. That would put a damper on the weekend. By now, I'm trying to guess which one it would be by the weight of the footsteps.

It must be Eric because he was heavier and this definitely sounded heavier. He made his way over to the iron staircase and I listened to see if he'd make it down without slipping, like I had done so many times during the week. Nope. No slipping. I not only heard, but I could feel the solid thud of each footfall on each metal step as he made his way down to the lower level. I am still pretending I'm sleeping when I hear the footsteps progress from the hallway straight into the bedroom where I was lying without the sound of a door opening. That was strange. I swore I had closed it before I took my nap. The footsteps now stopped at the bottom of the bed and I stubbornly held my position, waiting for him to say something and acknowledge that I was sleeping in their bed.

I took a few more breaths and finally turned around to face him, but there was no one to face. Again that old familiar feeling of having every hair on my body standing on end trying to understand just what was happening here. It was still early afternoon and plenty of light outside, so it's not like I couldn't see anyone standing there. There just was no one there.

I jumped out of bed and ran into the hallway. I checked the other bathroom and bedroom and outside, but those doors are still locked. I ran upstairs, but there was no one in the house. Those were heavy footsteps I heard and I could even feel the vibration of the steps while lying in bed. I thought maybe a burglar had walked in looking for something to steal, but someone that large could not have escaped that quickly and quietly without me knowing. This was something more. This might be the same guy that found my missing puzzle piece. If this ghost was helping me with my puzzle and being a good ghost, why scare the crap out of me by standing at the foot of my bed?

I sat fully awake in the living room until my friends finally made to the house. This time when I heard footsteps, I ran outside to make sure they were human. They were. Michael and Eric had arrived. I started to fly into my story about someone or something in the house and the missing puzzle piece and why are they both just standing there staring at me? Eric starts by telling me that this area of the Island was an Indian burial ground and that they hear stories like this one all the time. "Really?" I asked,

"Other people have missing puzzle pieces and then the pieces magically appear when no one is looking?"

He said, "No, not quite like that!" He assured me that they are harmless and just want people to know that they existed and had lived here. I thought that was pretty cool, actually. Instead of reading about Indians in a history book, Indian ghosts will actually come to your home to let you know that they're still around.

It wasn't totally terrifying for me since I still had all that previous ghost experience in my bedroom growing up. This could have been a test for me to see how I'd react this time and possibly not be totally frozen with terror. I think I passed. This ghost actually helped with my puzzle and had a purpose for being there. I would have liked to have asked him some questions before he disappeared but I think his message was delivered.

Chapter 4

LITTLE BILLY

1993

After the motorcycle accident offered me a new perspective on life, I noticed I was paying more attention to everything around me. I was finding myself outwardly grateful for things that were coming to me, and genuinely appreciative of each day I was able to wake up in my bed and say to myself, "I'm still here!"

I lived in a house in the famous 'Norma Triangle' area of West Hollywood. The story is that silent movie star, Norma Talmadge, had named all the streets after Hollywood stars. These tiny bungalows were also built for people who worked for the Los Angeles Pacific Railway, dating back to 1910. The little streets were charming and perfectly located between West Hollywood and Beverly Hills.

My house was a small 2-bedroom house with 2 baths and a small deck outside attached to the garage. Between the 2 bedrooms, there was a hallway that had a bathroom on one side and a floor to ceiling mirror that covered the opposite wall. It was always something I wanted to remove, but who wants to deal with the 7 years of bad luck you'd get for busting up a mirror? It also added a considerable amount of light to the hallway, so I left it up. The house was surrounded by trees, including this huge avocado tree right outside my bedroom. Many times during the night I'd wake up to the sound of squirrels fighting over a ripe avocado in their quest for a late night snack.

I had been in the house for a few years when I was given the terrible news about my young nephew who had unexpectedly died that morning. My brother and his wife live just outside Atlanta and had 2 girls, 4 and 8, and little Billy, who was only 6. Chicken Pox had something to do with his death along with some previous internal complications. My brother found him sleeping on the couch and when he went to pick him up, he died in his arms.

This extraordinary little guy was everything anyone would want in a son. He had brilliant blonde hair, beautiful blue eyes and the most amazing smiling dimples that would steal anyone's heart away. Billy was charming, smart and very good at sports. The one sport he excelled in was also my brother's passion, baseball. The whole family was thrilled when he made it to the cover of a Little League baseball card. My brother's passion for baseball was vicariously displayed every time little Billy played. His energy and joy were infectious and unstoppable.

My sister-in-law is a nurse so this personal tragedy was more than she should ever have to endure. I cannot imagine anything worse than a parent losing a child. The entire family was in shock for quite a long time. To keep his memory alive, his name was always added to the bottom of all holiday and thank you cards that were sent out for many years to follow.

We all start pounding our heads asking how could this happen and why. There can be no rational reason for a death that seemed so random. I believe our brain complicates matters with thoughts of fear, guilt, and blame, even when none of these fixations are accurate or relevant. If we are all placed on this earth for a reason and that reason is to learn something, it is possible that the lesson Billy was here to learn had been completed or the lesson he was to teach had been taught. Either way, it was an extremely painful lesson for those he left behind.

Four months later on a Friday night, I was looking forward to relaxing at home with a good book. I had finished dinner, showered and around 9:00 pm I jumped into bed. I turned on the bedside reading lamp, pulled the covers up and propped my book up in my lap. The house was quiet until about half an hour later. Very clearly, as I was totally engaged in my book, I heard a voice say, "Uncle Dicky!" I looked up from my book questioning what I had just heard. At first, I thought this must be an avocado falling onto the roof, or a squirrel playing outside, or a car horn, but this was exceptionally clear and loud. My brother's kids down in Atlanta were the only ones who called me Uncle Dicky and as far as I knew, I was in the house alone tonight. I know I did not imagine what I had just heard so, I looked around the room and with the house still quiet, I slowly got out of bed.

The rest of the house was dark so I walked over to the dimmer switch for the hallway light. I touched the knob and saw something move in the corner of my eye. As I turned my head toward the hallway, I saw little Billy standing there and started feeling that now familiar sensation of having every hair on my body standing on end, as well as a rush of emotion. At his center was this bright white light surrounded by a yellow aura. He stood flashing his brilliant smile and waving to me. By the time I had fully turned to see him, he had passed into the mirror and was gone. He left me with this intense tidal wave of love, joy, and gratitude. I never got the feeling that he was lost at all, but that he knew exactly where he was supposed to be. His message was that he was delighted in his new freedom, overjoyed, and satisfied that his message had somehow been delivered. He wanted me to know that, even if I wasn't totally sure of what his message was supposed to mean. There were no feelings of anger, regret, or unfinished business. I only felt his euphoria which lasted for over an hour even after he was gone.

I walked around the house to see if he might be hiding anywhere, but he was gone. I went back to my room and wrote down everything that had just happened along with the date and the time so I wouldn't forget anything. I sat there for what seemed to be an hour to two, trying to understand what I was feeling and why he showed himself to me and not his mom or dad. It took a long time for my heart to stop pounding in my chest before I could finally fall asleep. I held onto this information and did not tell anyone what had happened.

Sometime within the next year, my niece and I were emailing each other. Michelle was the second oldest and seemed to be in search of some answers. She was sending me some religious quotes that her mom had given her and asked what I thought. I told her that people have different beliefs and not everyone follows the same path. Religions offer people hope and strength to get through this tough life we are living. She asked me what I believed in and I said that I believe what I see. When she asked me what kind of things did I see, I told her I couldn't tell her. Now, you can never tell a budding teenage girl that you can't tell her something. That would drive them crazy, so I made her promise she wouldn't tell anyone else if I told her what I saw. She agreed and promised.

I described the whole event of sitting in bed, reading and hearing my name and what I witnessed and felt. She seemed upset after I told her what happened. I waited for a response. She thanked me for sharing the story with her and explained what a relief it was to hear that he was ok. What she conveyed to me was that since his death, both she and her older sister felt a degree of responsibility. Their thought was since they both had Chicken Pox before their brother contracted it, it must have been their fault when he also had Chicken Pox and died. It was a great relief for her to hear that he is fine, happy and doing well in his next level of existence. He wasn't angry or resentful with them and held no feelings of guilt or blame towards anyone.

It has taken me many years to realize that the things I see and feel are most likely not meant for me at all, but are to be shared and directed toward others. Now that I have had time to move past the fear they had all caused me, I understand the need to take the information I am given and pass it on.

Years later, after I shared this with my brother and his wife, Bill tells me that little Billy is back. He started recounting wonderful stories of things that would happen in their house. These were things that any 6-year-old boy would do to get someone's attention. Bill would be getting ready for work in the morning, walk into the kitchen and put his wallet down on the counter while finishing his coffee. He'd turn around to leave and his wallet would be gone. Checking his pockets, searching the floor and under the cabinets, back in the bedroom and bathroom, he'd find nothing. After half an hour looking and already late for work, he'd walk back into the kitchen and see his wallet exactly where he had left earlier that morning, in the middle of the counter.

This family really loved sports. Whenever their favorite team would score, along with all the yelling in the living room, they would notice the ceiling fan would turn on and the lights would flash. They would all sit and stare at it, knowing it was Billy showing his excitement, too.

My favorite story is about this solar carriage lantern I took with me after I sold my house. This was part of a collection of lamps I had on my front lawn. I had an extra one that I brought with me when I moved into my little apartment in Hollywood. I kept my lantern on my balcony where it could get some sun in hopes of being able to shine at night. It never did. I moved into a great new building downtown in the Arts District and still held onto that lantern. There it sits outside even as I write this, except that two years ago was different.

On the night of Dec 12th, as I was closing my bedroom blinds I noticed that my little lantern was burning brightly. I thought someone must have entered my apartment and put in real batteries and removed the old solar ones, or that it had a loose wire and had reconnected somehow. I went out and took pictures of the lantern with my cell phone to prove what I was seeing. I was thinking how nice it was to have my lantern working again and now everyone can see it down in the courtyard.

The next night as I was going to bed, I looked outside and saw no light. The lantern was there, just as it always had been, but it was not glowing like it did the night before. I took a picture of the non-working light, went to bed and would check it out tomorrow to find out why. The next morning I went outside, picked up the lantern and brought it into the kitchen. I wiped it clean, opened the top solar panel and found all the batteries were old and corroded. There was no way they would hold a charge after not working for almost 4 years! I checked the wires and connections but nothing gave me confidence that this light would ever light, even with new batteries.

When I sent the two pics out to my family, I received an immediate text back from my younger sister, Meg, who reminded me that December 13 was the anniversary of Little Billy's death. She suggested he was the only one who could make the lamp light up like it did. I thought that was wonderful and touching and I think of him now every time I look at my lantern. It has never worked again since that one night. Little Billy continues to let us know he's still around and we all find great comfort each and every time, knowing he's here.

Chapter 5

MOM HAS NOT
LEFT THE BUILDING

1996

My mother's side of the family always had this very special ability. No matter what you were trying to hide from my mom or grandmother, they'd see right through you as if your emotions were written right on your sleeve. I always thought it was magic. I was sure my mom knew magic, even if she only had one trick. She would place a dishtowel on the kitchen table. Then she'd have me close my eyes. When I opened them and lifted the towel, POOF! I would miraculously uncover a beautiful ripe plum. They were always the best plums because they were magic. She never made any other fruit appear. Only plums. It was like a "one-fruit-only" kind of magic trick, but I didn't mind.

The real magic that they shared was their empathetic connection. They had this great emotional insight to assume and share feelings, but it also gave them the vulnerability of being hypersensitive and always overly concerned about what other people think. In a society today where everyone can seem so self-centered and narcissistic by their constant Facebook and Instagram postings, there still are people around who may feel more than their fair share of hurt, pain, compassion, and love through their strong connection to other human beings. These are the sensitive ones that prefer to hide their emotions and not share with anyone how they truly feel in fear of being criticized for being too caring or too sensitive. We were raised to have to learn to be 'tough' in this world so we don't get walked over.

For some reason, there were suggestions that I may have been too loud as a child growing up in such a small house. I was always being told to "Quiet down! What will the neighbors think?" Why would I be concerned about what the neighbors think? They would probably think I was home and having fun. Would that be so horrible? This way of thinking was ingrained in us from a young age and continued throughout school. "What will the other kids at school think?" Mom would ask, and "What will your teachers think?" and "What will the priest think?"

I remember taking a class years ago that dealt with this very common issue. We were told to imagine ourselves on a very clear night, standing on top of the highest peak we could find. Looking up at the stars and over the city, we were to shout as loud as we could, pontificating all of our opinions about everything we considered important. We would shout out how we felt about our parents, siblings, friends, relationships, politicians, money, religion, world affairs, etc. Then we were asked to notice what happened next. Was there more activity in the city below? Did we experience any pain or discomfort? Did the earth or the stars move? No. Nothing happened.

An opinion is only a perspective thought, a belief, a perception or point of view of something and not necessarily based on fact. We do not have to accept the opinions of others. I imagine squeezing an opinion that was directed at me, into a little ball and returning it to the owner with love. "Thank you for your opinion, but this belongs to you and I think you should keep it", I'd say to myself. Once it has been returned to the owner, along with all of its negative energy, I am free and clear of it.

This hypersensitivity extended past just being concerned about other people's perceptions and opinions. This strong emotional connection allows us to easily feel and participate in the pain around us. We don't like seeing people hurt and it's difficult to observe suffering of any kind. Don't get me started on blood. It can be fake monster blood, war movie blood, television blood or real blood. Being too sensitive was annoying. It made me dizzy, nauseous and I would start to sweat and eventually pass out. I knew this reaction was all in my head and if I could just force my mind to think of other things, I'd be ok. If I could control it, I would not have any of the associated symptoms such as nausea, dizziness, and sweating. Easy, right?

High school was difficult because we started exploring the world in more depth and detail. In science class, we had to dissect a large frog. I remember the frogs were very rubbery and didn't seem like any of the real frogs I had seen by ponds and streams. I surely would have no problem cutting into this guy because he's probably all plastic inside anyway.

We each teamed up with a partner. One held the scalpel while the other took notes. I was feeling good about this, plus they didn't have any blood inside, so I should be fine. I took the knife and gently pressed it into the frog's belly. It gave way easily and began separating to reveal all the wonderfully organized internal organs. I always thought this was something that made girls squeamish, so I was constantly determined to fight any feeling that would show weakness, or that I was going to faint or pass out. Once the teacher started directing us in naming each of the organs, I began seeing white flashes and started getting lightheaded. I looked around and everyone seemed to be enjoying discovering all the internal bits. Why was I the only one starting to perspire?

I offered to switch out with my partner and take notes, and he excitedly jumped into action. Perfect timing. Now I could concentrate on note taking. I continued breathing deeply and trying to relax until our teacher mentioned something really cool. We could cut into the stomach and see what the little frog had been eating for dinner, just before he died. By the time our frog had revealed a bunch of squished flies inside the stomach, I was already excusing myself to head to the boy's room. I'll be right back. I just have to pee.

I headed out the door. Everyone was laughing and having a great time with this. I was sweating, nauseous and dizzy. I got to the bathroom and began splashing my face with cold water to try and lower my temperature. I sat down in one of the stalls and put my head between my legs to get my blood flowing back up to my brain. I did not understand why this constantly happened to me. There must be something wrong with my brain wiring. It's a frog. No one else is having an intense reaction like this. It is embarrassing, humiliating and probably dangerous, especially if I passed out and cracked my head on the marble floor!

By the time I pulled it together and headed back to class, they were done operating on all the frogs. They all said I missed the best part. "We got to dissect the eyeball! It was so cool!" my surgical partner reported. Ok. Got it. Didn't need to see that one. Everyone passed their tray of frog bits to the front of the classroom where they were all collected and we gathered up our belongings and headed off to the next class. I was fine as I was heading out, but just to test that this was really an issue and not something I ate, I started to think again about the frog's insides and slicing into the stomach and the eyeball and could feel the blood starting to leave my head again.

I went through the same thing the following year with the Driver's Ed Car Crash movie. Lots of bloody car accidents to terrify you into driving safely. Even though I would sit there with my eyes closed to avoid the gory scenes, my mind decided that it could create something even more spectacular in my brain by just listening to the sound of the crashes in the film. Closing your eyes doesn't make it better. Fortunately, these movies were never very long and I'd be able to pull myself back to normal before the lights came back on.

This inherited empathy has probably been passed down from generations before and continued through the rest of my family. I know my grandmother was empathetic, the same way my mom was. If my grandmother, mother, sisters, and brother had this empathetic ability, would my nieces and nephews have this also? I asked my sister's son if he ever felt he was oversensitive and that things would affect him more emotionally than other people and he said, "Yes! I thought there was something wrong with me!" We all got it. Even my nieces and nephews.

This empathy increased as I got older. I would sit in the movie theater and watch the audience's reaction during violent war scenes and no one would move. They didn't seem to be distressed at all. I would not be able to sit still. I'd be squirming in my seat feeling like I was inherently connected to the movie. At times I could smell someone smoking! I started looking around and could not believe someone would actually have a lit cigarette in the theater. I didn't see any smoke or illuminated cigarette tip until I looked onscreen. The actors in the movie were smoking and I am sitting here smelling it like some kind of scratch and sniff John Water's movie.

Whenever I'm in a situation that is causing anxiety, I try to disassociate myself from the source. For example, if I'm watching a movie and they are about to perform knee surgery on the lead actor, I can already anticipate my reaction. The knee is all propped up and even before they reach for the scalpel, the same feelings of light-headedness and nausea start to rise again. I try to distract myself by focusing on something else or closing my eyes.

The one thing that helps me is that I imagine an electrical cord that is plugged into my chest and entending into the movie screen. I just reach up and unplug this emotional cord from my chest. I tell myself that I will remain unattached and be able to watch the film the same as the rest of the audience is doing. Once I am separated emotionally from watching, I am able to relax and get through the remainder of the movie. For years, I would have to walk out and miss the rest of the film. Now I can at least work my way through to the end.

I needed to understand why I felt this way and started searching for answers. Empathy is defined as, "The ability to understand and share the mental or emotional state of another individual." Empathy can turn our emotions inward and become a self-inflicted pain, taking everything personally. Empaths will save everyone else first, before considering saving themselves and always feel responsible for the welfare of others. They believe everyone is good, which is not necessarily true. Empathy is all consuming, draining and can slowly erode us. It robs us of our own emotional experiences and forces us to take on someone else's. On the other hand, compassion turns our emotions outward in order to heal and is a way of being engaged, but distanced. What I try to do now is to use this empathetic information as an asset, change it into compassion and share it with those who can benefit. Do not take on and accept the pain. Empower yourself through the information you are receiving.

My grandmother, mother, and even my younger sister had turned their emotions inward as they never wanted to say or do anything that would upset anyone. The images I have of my mom are of her sitting at the kitchen table playing solitaire and smoking, or planted at the end of the sofa, watching television with a cigarette in her hand. As self-aware as my Mom was, my dad was the complete opposite. He loved people and interacted as often as possible. Although his humor was usually self-deprecating, he never seemed to care what others thought of him.

Such was my life, being torn between having dad's gregariousness and my mom's quiet super-sensitivity. My mom's smoking must have been hard on my dad and brother because they both had bad asthma and allergies and I'm sure this was not the best environment to be living in. I don't think any of us liked it, especially our new little sister who constantly pushed mom's overflowing ashtray away as she'd yell, "Ashes!" Mom never stopped and then in 1991, at 65 years old, was diagnosed with emphysema. This condition intensified over the next 5 years until she eventually died at 70.

Before I flew home from California, I heard she was asking for me from her hospital bed. She wanted me there because I could always make her laugh and I guess she needed to have her spirits lifted a bit. Maybe she knew that she was coming to the end of her life and wanted to leave with a smile on her face. I flew home and met the family, but not in time. Mom passed away before I arrived. We always try to prepare ourselves for the inevitable, but when it finally comes along we still are never really prepared.

The day of the funeral arrived and in the morning the immediate family is allowed to enter the funeral parlor to view the casket for the first time and have their private moments. I remember the whole family entering the building and feeling horribly nervous and sad and anxious and lost. The priest greets us and leads us inside. I was wondering what this was going to be like since I became so close to my grandmother after she died. I was hoping I could still have that same connection to mom now that she's gone, too.

We were a very close family so I just assumed this was going to be an incredibly difficult time for us all. I remember the door opening to a small room with a casket and not much else. There was a kneeling bench alongside the casket and my brother and sisters quickly knelt down while my dad and I stood. I was standing at the top and looking down, seeing a nice powder blue dress, her hands crossed over her chest and the ruby red ring she always wore still implanted on her finger. This blue dress was not one of mom's dresses, so someone arranged a wardrobe change for her.

As I leaned over even further, I noticed mom had a new hairstyle. This was considerably more poofie than she had even worn it, so it didn't really look like her. I wanted to reach down and touch her face to make sure she was real, but I didn't know if that was allowed. She had lost a lot of weight in the last few months so whoever fixed her up had applied lots of makeup. While I was in the middle of all of my observations, I heard everyone starting to cry. My mind was racing and trying to think of a kind way to tell everyone to calm down. This can't be our mom. They must have put her someplace else by mistake. Then I had an awful realization that I was not sharing the grief they were experiencing.

We were extremely close and yet I'm standing there feeling nothing towards this figure lying in the casket. I thought something was wrong with me. For some reason, I had become totally desensitized. I thought we all shared this amazingly strong empathetic bond, but mine wasn't working today, and I started to feel guilty and confused.

I thought it would be best if I just stepped to the back of the room and let them have their moment together. They could hold each other and share their grief while I remained out of the loop, embarrassed because I could not share their tears. I loved my mom deeply, but when I looked down into that box, I really did not know who that woman was. There was nothing representative of her except for her perpetually red painted fingernails and her ruby ring. I could not relate to the rest of what I saw. It was not only the visual information I was receiving, but the connection between us was gone. I could not feel her presence in the room. I tried thinking sad thoughts, but nothing worked. Mom had left the building.

Or so I thought. As I was standing against the far wall observing the scene, I felt something touch my right shoulder. As I turned my head to look, I felt a distinct squeeze along with an energy conveying a sense of reassurance. This was my mom placing her hand on my shoulder. She was still here and wanted me to know a few things before she left. I had that intense feeling of love and emotion washing over me again and in that moment she told me she was no longer in her body.

She explained that she had been living in her 'suitcase' and that she was leaving her suitcase behind now. She was happy and free to be back in her spiritual form once again. I was looking up at her because it always seems that our spirits are much larger when they are not crammed inside our smaller, carbon bodies. The emotions I was receiving were all about love, joy, and a feeling of relief and completion. She had suffered for the past five years and was filled with happiness to be free. She wanted everyone to know that this was where she was supposed to be now.

I actually said out loud, "There you are!" Upon hearing this, the rest of the family turned to me and asked me what I said. I told them that mom was over here with me and that she touched my shoulder. She wanted us to know that she is really happy, in a very good place and we shouldn't worry about her now.

My brother and sisters stood up and walked over to me along with my dad. As we were all huddled along the wall of the small room, we could smell her hair. This was the way my mom's hair always smelled all the time, not the way someone had fixed her hair after she left her suitcase. Mothers always have a scent. I don't mean that in a bad way, but most moms smell like moms whether it's their hair or lotion or perfume their scent is always recognizable. My mom always used the same hair spray and that's how I knew she was still here. This was a wonderful message of encouragement and we could all relax a bit knowing that she was no longer in pain and enjoying her new found freedom. How exciting!

We were still standing there by the wall when the priest knocked gently and walked back into the room. He stopped and looked at us, and then back at the casket. He asked us if anything was wrong. I think I said something like, "No, Father. Actually, everything is great. We just found out that she's not in her suitcase anymore!" The priest looked at us all a little peculiar as we filed out the door, but I'm sure he's seen stranger things than us in his years of doing this kind of work, so he refrained from asking any further questions.

The rest of the funeral was all by the book. When the mass and readings from friends and family members were completed, we carried the casket down the aisle to the big black car. We all jumped into our designated vehicles and followed it in procession to the cemetery where she was going to be buried. We all drove to this brick and glass building inside the cemetery where some last words were given and then I realized what the last step was going to be.

Inside the mausoleum, there were rows of these file drawers with marble covers all carved with names on them. Behind the marble coverings, were these sliding drawers containing corpses. How awful. How claustrophobic! I could never do that. That would be so uncomfortable. I wouldn't be able to breathe and that would be unacceptable. Afterward, I immediately wrote a living will requesting to be cremated and have my ashes disbursed inside every Disneyland property around the world. I needed to feel free and happy in the happiest places on earth!

I started a summer tradition after mom died. I'd fly back to Buffalo and rent a nice SUV, toss my dad and two sisters into the car and we'd start our journey. My dad's only surviving relatives at the time were his 2 sisters. His older sister was my Aunt Trudi who taught grammar school in Levittown, Long Island for many years. After she and my Uncle Bob retired, they moved to Chesterbrook, Pennsylvania, just outside of Valley Forge National Park. It was wonderful to see them together because even after so many years of marriage, they looked like two teenagers in love. Everywhere they went, they would be holding hands or my uncle would have his arm around my aunt's shoulder. Their move to Pennsylvania was a very special move because my aunt loved history and story telling and we'd spend a full day touring around old stone buildings where Washington himself had actually lived.

Trudi was tall and beautiful and I loved watching her tell us stories as a child. She was very animated with big hand gestures, a thick Long Island accent, dangling jewelry and crazy facial expressions that put me in ADD heaven! In addition to her many stories from teaching, she was afraid of everything; bugs, spiders, heights, driving, planes, boats, germs, you name it. Aunt Trudi would scream as she recounted the time Uncle Bob was driving too fast over some very high bridge and could not understand why was he driving in the lane closest to the edge where they would have a better chance of careening off the side and landing in the water below.

After spending a few wonderful days in Chesterbrook, we would drive up to Norwalk,

Connecticut to see my dad's twin sister, my Aunt Cile!
Twins share that great birth connection and always
know what the other twin is thinking. Cile would greet
us with open arms and even before we were
comfortably seated, she'd threaten to bring out the
dreaded photo albums!

My Aunt Cile and Uncle Bill loved cruising,
dancing and taking lots and lots of pictures. Her
favorite story was while she was ballroom dancing
with my Uncle Bill on one of their many cruises, they
were approached by one of the members of the Arthur
Murray Dance Studios and asked if they'd be willing
to be instructors at the studio. My Aunt was so
immensely flattered that I'm sure that made their
cruise one they would never forget.

As we prepared for bed that night, we had to
make sleeping arrangements in her small 3-bedroom
home. She lived alone after her husband died and my
cousins grew up and moved out. My Aunt took one of
the smaller rooms and dad slept in a twin bed in the
guest room. My sister and I shared the master bedroom
with the queen-sized bed. I was so tired at that point,
that I remember jumping into my boxers and t-shirt
and grabbing the left side of the bed closest to the door
in case I had to get up and pee during the night.

My sister, Judy, was in her nightgown and
taking out her contacts when she heard me talking
quietly. I was lying on my back with the blankets

pulled up to my chin and when I closed my eyes, I felt and saw my mom bending over me, kissing me on my forehead and saying goodnight. I responded by saying, "Thank you. Goodnight Mom!" That's when Judy heard me and asked who I was talking to. I told her mom was here saying goodnight. As she walked over to my side of the bed, we could smell that familiar scent of my mother and knew mom was in the room right now. It was such a wonderfully comforting feeling knowing that she is still around looking out for us. We both slept deeply that night and woke up to the sound of dad and his sister singing some of their old favorites from the dining room table.

After breakfast, we shared the story of mom's visit last night. This was not an unusual conversation in our household. We'd often talk about spirits and ghosts and strange things that would happen that we would blame on some dead relative. I like to say they're like helium balloons attached to strings. I can pull them down to see how they are doing, if they need anything or if they have any messages for rest of the family, and then release them back up to where they were.

One of my Aunt's favorite shows was "The King and I" and her favorite song to dance to was "Shall We Dance". Cile would fire up the old stereo record player in the living room, put the record on and start dancing with her arm on top of Bill's invisible shoulder while holding his hand in hers. She'd dance around with him and you could see the sheer joy spread across her face as we all applauded our approval. What a wonderful way to keep a memory alive.

You can imagine my shock when I went to see Meryl Streep in "The Iron Lady" about Margaret Thatcher and there in the beginning of the film she is dancing with her arms around her dead husband to, of all things, "Shall We Dance"! I thought I was seeing things. Could this be a popular thing to do for widows to keep them from being lonely? The big difference was that Cile did not have Alzheimer's and she was never a Prime Minister. Maybe I should try Googling the writers to see if any of them knew my aunt or lived nearby and were peeping into her windows late at night watching her dance.

Mom, dad, Trudi, and Bob are all helium balloons now and Aunt Cile is alive and kicking at 93 taking care of the nursing home residents in Connecticut to make sure they are not late for karaoke, bingo, sing-a-longs and all the dances they have there on a regular basis. I love my family!

Chapter 6

THE CARRIAGE HOUSE

2000

I bought what I was always told to buy, the ugliest house on the street. At this point, I was not really considering the distinct advantage of having ghosts on the property, but I was still learning. This was a totally run-down 1910 Craftsman house with three bedrooms and one little bathroom but with another very nice feature. In the back was the original horse stables and above them, the carriage house. These all-wooden structures were in great need of repair, lots of upgrades, a new coat of paint and a lot of love. Every time I would drive by and show my friends which house I considered buying, they would respond with, "You can't be serious!" or "You are joking, right?" It looked like the house had been picked up by some big twister in the Midwest and dropped right here on this street full of apartment houses in West Hollywood. To me, it was like the Charlie Brown Christmas Tree. It just needed a little love!

The sister property of this house was built at the same time but had burned down years ago leaving an empty lot. There were very few of these original Craftsman homes left as large apartment buildings were moving in and taking over. I was determined to bring it back to its original structure and appearance. The place had good bones.

The main house was only 900 square feet and still had all of the original wooden flooring. There was a 3-foot square cut into the floor where the wood had been replaced. The story I was given was that the original owner was a smoker who fell asleep one night in his favorite armchair, set himself on fire, and died. The chair was destroyed and burned the flooring beneath it, which is why it had been replaced.

As I was growing more intuitive about my spiritual surroundings, I never felt that the ghost of this man had stayed in the house. Not all spirits that transition choose to stay in the place where they died. Most move on and go wherever they are supposed to go. Those spirits that choose to stay around and are either stuck or lost are what I refer to as ghosts.

This place had a great deal of history and I didn't want any of it to disappear. I wanted to refresh it and make it new again. I love working with wood. This once-living building material retains its energies and allows new ones to penetrate. Even my furniture was all wood. I had a beautiful 100-year-old English spindle dining table, a solid wood coffee table, desks, buffet, end table, and lamps. All of my things have that same warm, receptive energy and since trees were all well rooted, the energies are very grounding for me.

There was a great deal of work to be done and I like doing as much of it as possible myself. The entire bathroom had to be replaced and most of the kitchen. I did all of my own painting, woodwork, tile work and landscaping. I found it very relaxing as well as a great creative outlet. I always had some of my friends around who would volunteer to help out, so I can't actually say that I did it all myself.

This area of Hollywood was famous for its ghost stories. Just up the street was the famous Viper Room where the ghost of River Phoenix has been seen frequently. Then there are all the stories from the Comedy Store, Barney's Beanery, the Magic Castle, hotels and restaurants that hold all the history of Hollywood. I felt that the front house had a great energy, but the back units were a different story.

The tenant who lived downstairs had been living there for over 30 years. He was already 90 years old and an amazing man. His father was the original gardener for the Beverly Hills Hotel and had bought up most of the orange groves in the area. He showed me a picture of the intersection of Santa Monica and San Vicente Boulevards where both were just dirt roads with hitching posts on the corner to tie your horses to.

His dad had sold off the land a long time ago and all that Ray was left with were the few things inside the converted horse stable. He enjoyed gardening like his father did. Several times a week, usually at 5 am, I'd hear him outside my bedroom window with his hedging shears clipping away at the bushes alongside the house. The man was in amazingly good health for his age until one day he just wandered off. I found out the next day that he ended up in the hospital because he did not remember how to get home and had fallen off a curb. Ray passed away quietly at 93 years old after an amazingly free and happy life.

The tenant in the upstairs unit decided to move out and I had a great opportunity to get inside and do a full renovation. The elevated one bedroom apartment was like having your own home. This great space had two separate entrances and 12 windows that had unobstructed views in each direction.

I began filling the large living room closet with all the materials I was planning on using in the space. I had buckets of paint, wallpaper, a large collection of left over tile, wood trim, lighting and even a new fireplace mantle still in its original box. Walking around this space had a totally different feel than the one down below. I distinctly had the feeling that I was being watched. Initially, I thought it was because of all the windows, but the more time I spent up here and the more I experienced all of my hair standing on end, I knew I was not alone.

I had planned on starting in the kitchen with all new tile countertops and flooring, so I went up to the unit one night to see just how many tiles I actually had. I turned on the bare bulb light in the closet and looked inside. There was the fireplace mantle leaning up against the back wall of the closet and the floor was filled with all of my past renovation materials. I pulled up the only chair, a white plastic lawn chair, and under the dim light, I began counting my leftover floor tiles. I had a note pad so I could write down how many more tiles I would need to finish the kitchen floor.

As I was writing numbers down on my pad, the mantle decided it needed some attention so from its comfortable leaning position against the wall, it somehow straightened and then fell down directly on my head. I was a bit stunned to see the mantle on the floor and wondered for a second just how it came to rest in front of me, hitting my head along the way. At that point, I distinctly felt another presence in the house.

I stood up and said out loud, "Ok, now. That was not funny. If I had hurt myself, there would be no one around to fix up this place, so you'd have to do it yourself. Please don't do that again." I was getting a feeling of playfulness along with a satisfaction that he had my attention and that I acknowledged him. This was a young spirit, a male, about 11 years old. The things that he continued to do during the renovation were very age-appropriate and I'd correct him each time. As I left the apartment, I returned the mantle to its upright position, turned off the light and closed the closet door. I left the chair in the living room, facing the windows and told the boy if he gets tired, he could sit here and look out the window tonight, and to please behave himself. As I left, I locked the door to the apartment, walked down the wooden stairs and my back to my house for the night.

In the morning, I made my single cup of coffee as usual and headed outside towards the unit once again. I needed to take some additional measurements of the countertops before heading out to Home Depot and wanted to get an early start. I walked back up the stairs and unlocked the door to the unit. I stood there staring at the chair I had left in the living room distinctly facing the windows, except now it was turned around and facing me. I even went to the back door to make sure it was locked, thinking someone might have snuck in here during the night and played with my chair. It, of course, was locked and secured. At least I thought it was going to be nice having some company while renovating. I just wish he was able to hold a paint brush and help paint!

After running out to the store for supplies, I could focus on the floor. The original flooring had to be removed before I could start on the tile. I brought up an old radio I had, with the thought that some music would help make the job a little more pleasant. I plugged it in and searched for a clear station. The best one I could find was an oldies station that I could sing along to while I worked.

Everything was going smoothly and a few days later I could actually begin laying the tiles. On the morning I started putting the cement on the floor and placing the tiles, I thought something was missing. I forgot to turn on the radio, which was sitting in the living room. Simultaneously as the thought entered my head, I heard the radio click on in the living room. I could hear some static as it began to search for a station. Once he found it, the music came in loud and clear. I thanked him for helping me out and continued singing along to the songs I was familiar with. I never thought to ask him the questions that I later learned to ask in these situations. Are you happy here? Is there someplace else you'd rather be? Do you have any other family members over there that you'd like to see?

I ended up hiring a team to help finish the renovation to be able to get the work completed on time. I found a nice tenant who never even asked if there was a ghost in the apartment before she signed the lease. I would have had to charge her more rent if they both planned on sharing the space, so I never mentioned it.

He seemed happy there, and I never got the feeling that he was angry or lost. Even after I sold the property, I'd go drive by it and look up at the windows in the back to see if maybe he was still there, playing with the blinds or throwing things. I never saw or felt him there after that. I hope he found out where he was supposed to go. I guess sometimes they just want to be noticed, even if takes hitting you over the head with a mantle.

Chapter 7

THE HOTEL IN SAN FRANCISCO

2006

What started out as just a group of friends being invited to San Francisco for a birthday party weekend, turned into another enlightening encounter. Once I committed myself to going, my next step was to find the perfect place to stay. I love old architecture and history, and San Francisco has so many of these places to choose from. Even in my renovation work, I always searched for properties that have some history and good bones. I found this great boutique hotel chain that renovated old pre-existing properties. The one I liked was centrally located and the pictures of the hotel looked perfect.

We flew up to San Francisco and BART took us within walking distance of the hotel. I remember crossing the street and gazing up at the facade of this old Victorian home and just knew it had to be haunted! The pictures of the rooms online were almost a bit like someone's grandmother had done the decorating, but I understood they were maintaining the integrity of the property.

We climbed the stairs and entered into the foyer to find a small welcoming vestibule that contained a very helpful concierge. I was hoping for a room on one of the upper floors and was slightly disappointed to find out our room was downstairs. He assured me it was one of the larger rooms in the hotel and even had its own fireplace. On the way to the elevator, the nice man informed me that this hotel was a "walk-up", meaning there was no elevator. That was fine. I can handle walking down a flight of stairs.

I inserted the key card into the door lock, opened the door and entered the room. My first impression was that it was unusually cold in here. We were actually underground and only had small basement windows that would allow us to see outside. Now I understood why we needed a fireplace here. It must get even colder down here at night. I have always been more than a little claustrophobic when it comes to putting me in small places, much less underground. I was trying to reassure myself that we wouldn't be spending much time here so it didn't matter what floor we were on.

As I began to unpack, I couldn't help shake this uncomfortable feeling of being closed in, so I climbed back up the stairs to talk to the concierge. I told him it was really a very nice room, but I'd really appreciate something that wasn't underground. He told me the hotel was almost full and the only other room that was available was on the top floor. I was excited to hear we would be above ground and possibly have a view of the city. I said that sounded perfect. He told me the room was on the 5th floor. "Are you sure you want to be on the 5th floor?" the concierge asked. I assumed he meant because we'd have to walk up all 5 floors. I told him that would be fine and I'd love to see it. He reached up to the wall, pulled a key off a hook and as he handed it to me, he said, "Then the 5th floor it is!" I said a very appreciative thank you and swore I heard a muffled, "Good luck" as I was heading downstairs.

We climbed up the 5 flights of old carpeted, wooden stairs and reached the landing a bit winded from hauling our bags. The long hallway was charming and very much like someone's grandmother was up here decorating, too. On one side of the hallway was a series of windows with a view that was much better than what we had down below in the basement. This felt so much more open up here, plus we were on the top floor. The penthouse, sort of!

The room was not as large as the one in the basement, but it was warmer and had a great window. We quickly unpacked, showered, and got ready to head over to the birthday party. The late afternoon air was moist and crisp, almost on the verge of being cold.

We weren't standing still for very long and walking around San Francisco was invigorating. By the time we reached the party, I was just about ready for bed. After all, this was a full day of travel, climbing stairs and running through San Francisco already. I said all my hello's and birthday greetings and was hoping that this wasn't going to be a late party!

I stayed for a few beers and when it was suggested that the group was ready to move on and hit some of the local clubs, I created the perfect excuse to bow out. I told them I was on a mission to see just how comfortable those beds in the hotel were going to be. The cab driver knew exactly where I was staying and once I got inside the hotel entryway, I discovered a new concierge sitting in the box.

I said hello and explained how tired my legs were from all the walking and asked if the concierge would kindly carry me up to the 5th floor. He was able to deny my request by offering to share his bad back story with me. Then he laughed and asked, "So, you're staying up on 5?" I told him I was and that we were originally booked into the basement, but it was scary down there. I didn't want to be sleeping underground. He laughed again and wished me good luck climbing the stairs and as I started up, I heard, "And sweet dreams!" I thanked him and concentrated on the five flights ahead of me.

I was pleased to have made it up without having a coronary and headed down the long hallway to the room. After brushing my teeth, washing my face, I poured myself into bed. It was still only 11:30 pm and I'm sure I was fast asleep by 11:31 and nothing was going to wake me up at this point.

My deep sleep didn't last very long. I woke up when I heard someone running down the long hallway, bounding off the walls and probably very drunk. I thought for a quick second that I was so glad I was not in the same state and went to bed when I did. The next thing I heard took me by surprise. Whoever was running had tripped and fallen with a loud CRASH!, right against my door! I thought they must have done some real damage if not to the door, then to themselves. I jumped out of bed and quickly ran over to the door and opened it.

There was no one passed out on the floor. There was no one standing by the door. The frame and woodwork of the door were all fine, so I leaned out of the room and peered down the long hallway. There was no one in sight. My room was at the end of the hallway with no other exit, so whoever fell had no place to go or hide. I stood there for a long while listening to see if there was some important piece of information I was missing here. All was quiet again so I closed and locked the door and climbed back into bed. I pushed all the thoughts of what had just happened out of my head and was able to fall back asleep.

About an hour later I woke up again after hearing a distant, loud BANG! I sat up and listened carefully, making sure I was fully awake this time. Starting at the far end of the hall, I could hear the same loud footsteps running towards my door again. I sat for a second in disbelief, but this time I intended to jump out of bed fast enough to catch whoever it was before they fell into my door again. By the time my feet hit the floor, I heard the same loud CRASH! against the door! I flung the door open immediately afterward and stepped outside the door, once again observed the site of an empty hallway.

I stood there realizing some ghost must think it's funny to play games like this at night and wake people up. I stood in the hallway and spoke to it directly, "All right, you have my attention now. Is there anything else you need from me? If not, then we are finished here and I'm going back to sleep. Please do not wake me up again!"

I walked back inside the room and closed the door. What an odd game to play and what possibly could the message be here, unless he just wanted attention by running down the hall and smashing against a door. I was still very tired, so I went back to bed and slept through the rest of the night.

I woke up the next morning to a beautiful, clear San Francisco day. Steve made it back to the room safely and was still asleep in the next bed. I showered and got dressed and headed down to the wonderful continental breakfast that the hotel offered every morning for its guests. What exactly makes a breakfast continental and which continent are they referring to?

I researched it later to find out that a continental hotel breakfast may include sliced bread with butter/jam/honey, cheese, meat, croissants, pastries, rolls, fruit juice and various hot beverages. It is served commonly throughout continental Europe, as opposed to the English breakfast served in the UK or a traditional American breakfast. Who knew? So there I was having my continental fruit and coffee when my friend, Steve joined me and was able to fill me in on all the fun I missed out on the night before.

We would be leaving the hotel later in the afternoon, so I wanted to get out and see as much as we could on this beautiful day. After gulping down our continental coffee (which was probably Folger's) we exited the dining area and were passing the little area where the concierge sits.

"How was your night?" he asked. I turned to see that it was our original host from yesterday when we checked in. My knee jerk response was, "It was great, thank you. How was yours?" He told us he was just at home relaxing but proceeded to ask me how I slept. I said, "Oh, I always sleep like a rock and the beds were really comfortable."

"So, you didn't wake up at all last night?" he asked. As soon as asked that, I had a total flashback of what happened last night. I had been so busy waking up and packing that I forgot about my visitor. Is he hinting that this is something he was aware of?

I responded, "Well, now that you mentioned it, I did wake up a few times last night. Why do you ask?"

He looked around to see if anyone else was within earshot and said, "It's just that some of the guests swear that they hear someone running down the hall at night…"

And I followed up with, "… and falling into my door?"

"Yes", he answered. "It's always the same thing every night and falling into the same door."

"So, that's why you asked me if I was ok with staying the 5th floor! Why didn't you tell me before we checked in there?"

"Well, not everyone hears him and you never know how a guest is going to respond with having to share a hotel with a ghost. He's only on that floor and most people don't complain about the noise, or maybe they just deny that it happens at all."

"I think he needs to expand his routine unless maybe he's repeating a message for us. That might be how he died. He could have come back to the hotel drunk that night. Maybe he had to pee, so he started running down the hall. Before he reached his room, he tripped and fell head first into the doorframe, smashed his head, and died! Now he just wants everyone to know how his life ended. At least he's doing that with a purpose!"

"That would make sense. The next time I'm up there, I'll ask him" he said and smiled.

I was still curious, "So, why don't you advertise the hotel as a haunted hotel? Wouldn't that be an asset? You'd probably have lines of people waiting outside just to book a room! Unless there's too much competition for that."

"Yes! There are so many old hotels in San Francisco that have ghost stories, and don't forget Alcatraz and the Golden Gate Bridge!" he added. I signed for our room, grabbed my bag and thought, at least the ghost is not hurting anyone and he seems to be enjoying his nightly task.

"Thank you again for a memorable experience!" I said, "Maybe this story will appear as a chapter in someone's book some day!" As we turned and headed for the door, he bid us farewell and wished us a safe flight. What a wonderful education this one was. I seem to be getting more comfortable with having them around me. Next step would be to see if I could start communicating with the spirits that aren't family. It would be nice to find out why they are there and what they are hoping to gain by their presence.

Flying back to Los Angeles and then grabbing a cab back to my latest home renovation project, a 1927 English Tudor castle facing the park. This was a beautiful 3-story home with a turret on a private street surrounded by a park and trees. I spent seven years at this property and it proved to be the most haunted one yet!…

Chapter 8

ANNA ELIZABETH MARIE

2006

How do you market a haunted house? I just personally thought that having a house that was haunted would increase the value due to a lack of similar properties on the market. Doesn't everyone want to live in a haunted house? You'd never be alone and there would always be someone around to talk to and keep you company. Then there's the added benefit of having a security system of ghosts in the house and you don't even have to pay them for their services. Anytime someone is trying to break in, they just start slamming doors or turning the lights and TV on and off. Any sane criminal would flee without even thinking twice. Yes, I think people would definitely be willing to pay more for a haunted house.

When I first saw the house, it was so hidden by an overgrowth of trees that all I could see was a portion of the garage door and the balcony above. The listing sounded interesting and I wondered why it had been on the market for so long. Anyone that has ever gone house hunting knows what happens when you find the perfect house. It tugs at your intuition and you just get a feeling, a knowing, that this is the right house for you. Well, this house let me know in more ways than one.

I made an appointment with the realtor to see the house and parked my car in front. Looking up from the tree lined private street, to the gradual sloping driveway leading to the front door of the stately 3-story home, all seemed perfect. Within a few seconds of walking into the house and entering into the grand living room, I instantly knew that I would be the next owner and that there would be some valuable life lessons ahead for me. I tried to remain calm while the realtor showed me around, but I was already picturing myself living here and what I would do differently to make the house my own.

The grand living room had 23-foot high ceilings with 10-foot high French doors opening out to a balcony that overlooked the front yard, curved driveway, and a huge Japanese magnolia tree. This magnolia was one of the largest I've ever seen of its kind and people would come from all over just to stand under the flowering tree and take pictures. There was 1 bedroom downstairs with 3 more upstairs and because the house was cut into the hillside, there were exit doors to the outside from every floor. I thought that would be convenient in case of a fire. I would never have to worry about being caught on the top of the turret yelling for help or having to jump out of a 3rd-floor window into the rose bushes far below. I could just exit one of the back doors.

The deal went through and I was able to close escrow after all the inspections were completed. I called the house my castle because it was, with a little imagination, very castle-like. The house was already empty, so I was able to move in quickly and began getting settled in my new home. After a few nights of adjusting to sleeping in such a large house alone, Los Angles was hit with an enormous rainstorm. At least I would have a chance to see just how sturdy the house is and if there were any water leaks.

I was sound asleep and some time in the middle of the night, the storm hit. We actually had thunder and lightning, which we almost never get out here in California. The house was surrounded by very tall trees that I thought would add some protection during a storm. In reality, it only made the house extremely dark and along with the loud noise of the tree branches beating against the sides of the house, made it very unsettling. It must have been close to 4:00 am when I heard a large crash outside and then complete darkness. All of my nightlights and little electronic diodes were out. The house was wired with an alarm system that had connectors attached to each window and door and when the contact was broken, an annoying little computer voice would tell you which entry was compromised.

There was no light source from anywhere inside or outside the house and I thought this is what it must be to be completely blind. The house was still new to me, so I didn't want to go running through the hallways blindly, trip and fall and go flying head first over the balcony. I'll just sit here and wait for the electricity to come back on again. The next thing that happened made me just about jump out of my skin.

All I could hear was the wind blowing and banging tree branches against the house, but then there was a voice. A voice right here in my bedroom while I was in a state of complete blindness. The voice was loud and clear and said, "Bathroom window open!" What? I realized it was the annoying computer voice of the security system telling me a connection had been opened. Which bathroom? There were four bathrooms in the house and how was this computer voice even working with no electricity?

Ok. Think. There must be an emergency generator or battery attached to the alarm system in case of a power outage. That would make sense and helped me to calm down a bit. The only problem was that every few minutes the alarm voice would repeat, "Bathroom window open!" Does that mean that someone was breaking into my house during a storm? The house had been vacant for a long time and any local burglars would have noticed that the house was for sale, presumably with no one inside and with all the lights out, they might still believe the house was empty.

I didn't have anything that would serve as a weapon to defend myself from any intruders. I could lock my bedroom door and hope that would be enough of a deterrent unless they were breaking into the master bathroom right next to me! I had to do something fast. Sitting in complete darkness while someone is breaking into your new home is a bit unnerving, to say the least. I needed time to think.

I always kept flashlights around in case of emergency. I wondered if I had I thought enough in advance to stash one in the nightstand while unpacking. I rolled over to the other side of the bed and fumbled for the handle on the nightstand drawer, grasped it and pulled it open. As I reached inside, I was wondering how the drawer was already full of stuff when I had just moved in here, but then there, in the back of the drawer, I felt it.

It was one of those small metal LED flashlights that had an impressive number of lumens, whatever a lumen was. They came in a four pack encased in an indestructible plastic packaging from Costco that could only be opened with a blowtorch or a small set of explosives. It should also come with a pack of Band-Aids for everyone who has ever cut themselves while trying to open these things.

I pulled the flashlight out of the drawer and hoped it also had batteries in it. I pressed the button and saw my bedroom illuminate in both light and shadows, while the computer voice kept reminding me that there was still someone or something opening a window somewhere. I jumped out of bed and slowly walked over to the master bathroom and pointed the light up to the small window over the jacuzzi tub. This window could be accessible from the outside because the 3rd floor had a full landing around it. This bathroom was intact and that left three more to check out.

As I passed the master alarm system that continued to yell at me, I murmured a quick, "Please, shut up!" Evidently, my request was ignored, so I proceeded to open my bedroom door to the balcony above the living room. I had just moved in, so at this point, the living room was still equipped with these hideous gold earring chandeliers. As ugly as they were, I would have appreciated them much more if they were working right now.

As I walked across the balcony to the upstairs guest bathroom, I realized that bathroom window would be impossible to break into since it was 2 stories above ground. That left the living room bathroom or the bathroom down on the first floor by my office. It most likely would be the window off the living room, which would be very accessible by walking up the stairs alongside the house.

I started thinking as I was walking down the stairs that if someone was down there and it was only me in the house in my underwear and tee-shirt, I wouldn't stand a chance if they had a weapon. What if the burglar thought there was more than one person in the house? Maybe that could work to my advantage. So I began calling for different names in house and using different voices and answering myself while waving the flashlight around wildly making anyone think that there was more than one flashlight now.

"Hey, Jeffrey! Where are you now, and where is Rita? Is she with you?" Deepening my voice I replied, "No, Rodger! She's not up here. She must be downstairs with Brian!" "Ok! I'll look for them down here. Is Paul still down there in the basement?" I asked loudly. "Yes! I think he's down there with Denise!" I yelled in my best Rita-voice.

I continued yelling and waving the flashlight around as I crossed the living room floor to the closed door of the bathroom. I took a deep breath as I put my hand on the knob and gave it a turn. I yelled out a great big, "Whoo-hoo!" as I pulled the door open and looked inside. I felt an enormous wave of relief rush over me as I looked up at the window and found no one there. The top portion of the window was not latched so the wind must have blown it open, breaking the connection, and sounding the alarm.

That meant there was no burglar and I wasn't going to die in my new house. This was reassuring as I pushed the window shut, turned the latch and heard a final announcement from the computer voice upstairs. I turned and left the bathroom, shutting the door behind me, gratified that I had solved the problem of the open window. For a brief moment, I was concerned that one of my neighbors may have heard me yelling and screaming and waving a flashlight around while running through the house in my underwear. What an introduction that would have made!

I survived the storm, but this storm added considerably to the amount of water damage the house had suffered over the years. The main supporting wall in the living room had wood rot and had to be replaced, as well as the roof, balcony, and most of the garage beneath.

I was still living in the house during the renovation when the contractors had removed the entire roof and the main wall facing the street. It made it very difficult to go from the master bedroom at one end of the house, across the upstairs living room balcony to the guest bathroom at the far end of the house. I just preferred showering in the smaller bathroom because it was easier to use and keep clean than the large master tub with the large bay windows.

So, I'd wake up in the morning, take off my clothes and wrap one of my favorite thirsty bath towels around my waist. The stores always advertised certain thick bath towels as being 'thirsty', like someone was depriving them of water for some reason. I guess the thought was that if you were wet, these thirsty towels would suck up all the water drops on your body, leaving you dry and exfoliated, as the thirsty towels would be plump and full of water and no longer thirsty.

Anyway, this morning as I grabbed the bedroom door handle and pulled it open, I stepped through the doorway wearing only my thirsty bath towel and suddenly I heard voices in my living room. As I looked down, I realized they weren't actually in my living room, but standing outside under my Japanese magnolia tree. One of the keen-sighted tourists happened to be looking up and since there was no wall or roof, spotted me running towards the guest bathroom and yet felt compelled to yell, "Hey, look! There's a naked man running up there!"

I was not naked. I was wearing a thirsty bath towel, which I guess he forgot to mention during his announcement. I remember showering and thinking of different ways I could return to the master bedroom without being witnessed and accused of being naked again. I could exit the guest room to the rear terrace, head around back to the side of the house and hope that the sliding doors into the bedroom were unlocked. I'm sure they would be locked. I always kept them locked. Fine. It looks like I'll have to take a chance and hope that the group outside had moved on and weren't waiting for me to finish my shower so they could snap some pics!

I dried myself off, wrapped my towel around my waist again, peered around the door and looked outside. I just caught sight of the last few stragglers in the group as they were leaving to go inspect another area of the park. I decided to run back to my bedroom anyway, just in case. Something else startled me as I was running. There were two birds in the rafters looking to make my open roof their next nesting location. They were probably chirping to each other, "Look! There's a naked human running after us!" I would have chirped back to them and told them that I again, was not naked.

Introducing Anna.

It wasn't long after that when I realized I was not alone in the house. In my previous properties, I always had tenants or roommates. This was the first time I can remember living alone. I knew the house needed work and I thought it would be better not to have anyone else living here during the renovation. Well, there was someone else here and at first, it was just that feeling that someone was watching me.

Besides the master bedroom, I had two guest bedrooms upstairs. The back bedroom had a queen-sized bed, faced my neighbor to the north and had doors that opened to the back landing of the property facing west. The other bedroom faced the park from the 3rd floor and also had windows facing north. This room had the best views out of any other room in the house and my guests here didn't seem to mind sleeping on the comfy couch. The one thing that did seem to bother them was that something would happen to anyone who chose to stay in that room and always occurred at the same time every night.

One morning at breakfast and soon after I had moved in, my first guest to stay there asked me if I had turned on the air conditioner during the night. I said that I rarely use the air conditioner because living in this area and so close to the park, there is always a natural coolness in the air every night. He said that was strange because he remembered waking up during the night from a cool breeze blowing across his face. I thought nothing of it until the next time someone stayed there and reported the same thing to me. This time my guest had looked at his watch and remembered the time was 3:30 am.

This went on for as long as I lived in the house. At precisely 3:30 am each guest that stayed in that room would feel a cool breeze blowing across their face, enough to wake them up. That was just one of many things that made my house very special. Add that to the list of amenities. Free air conditioning!

After living in the house for a few months, I would wake up to the sound of voices in the living room. At first, I thought it was coming from outside as if one of the neighbors was having a party. My house was on a private street that was not well lit, so there were never any people just out for a casual stroll. I climbed out of bed and walked over to my bedroom door to listen. I had no houseguests staying with me, so I was getting very concerned about who was having a conversation in my living room. I opened the door and leaned over the balcony and saw the glow of the television illuminating the sofa and coffee table down below. The TV was on. Ok, fine. I'll just go turn it off. I assumed there might have been some kind of power surge somewhere that was strong enough to turn it on. I shut off the TV and returned to bed.

It wasn't much of an incident nor was it important enough to even mention to anyone else, until it happened again the following week. The same kind of voices woke me in the middle of the night and I'd open my door and see that the TV was on. I said out loud, "Really? This is how you choose to entertain yourself, by turning on my television?" So, I walked down the stairway, crossed the living room to the remote sitting on the coffee table and picked it up. I aimed the remote at the TV and pressed the power button and the TV turned black. I put the remote back on the table, turned and headed back up the stairs.

I only got about half way up the stairs when the TV turned back on again. This time I could feel the hair on my arms and neck begin to stand up and I said, "Ok. That was impressive, but all I have to do is turn it off again", which I did, and started back up the stairs one more time. I got half way up and once again the TV turns on and I was beginning to get upset over this. I said, "Ok, now. Stop it now, please."

I remembered the boy ghost I had in my carriage house and what I told him at the time, "If you are really able to do this, why can't you put your energy into something productive like cleaning the windows and floors instead of turning on my TV in the middle of the night?" I turned it off again and as I headed up the stairs, I paused and said, "I'm going to bed now and I don't want to hear any more, so please behave yourself. Now, good night!" I walked back upstairs, shut my door and went back to bed and slept soundly for the rest of the night.

I intuitively began receiving information about who I was sharing the house with. I knew it wasn't an adult because the things that were happening would be something that a child would do to get attention. I felt that this was the spirit of a little girl. She was about eight years old with long light brown hair. Her energy never felt malicious or bad in any way, but more along the line of being curious about almost everything I was doing in the house. All my friends, housemates and even family that stayed with me, had the pleasure of experiencing my friendly house ghost and sharing in the stories.

I thought as long as she wasn't causing any trouble or disturbing my sleep, what harm could there be in letting her stay? Everything was fine until the following week. I woke up to the sounds of a party going on. She's at it again, I thought, but this time it sounded different. There was music and laughing and people singing… in my living room?

I was thinking the best way to end this from now on was to just unplug the television before I go to bed each night and then I wouldn't have any more interruptions. This was getting tiresome, so I opened the door and walked quickly down the hallway, but as I turned and started down the stairs, I noticed there were no lights on from the TV this time. Just as quickly, all the sounds of the party ceased and I was standing silently on the stairs looking at nothing. I wanted to let her know that this was not ok, but finding the right words took me a minute or two.

"This is unacceptable and I have to put my foot down. I'm sorry. Please thank them for coming, and ask them nicely to leave because the human in the house needs to sleep. We will discuss this tomorrow, young lady! Good night." I said as I went back upstairs and crawled into bed.

The next day, I thought about the conversation I had with the little girl in the house. Maybe ghosts do listen and maybe they are able to communicate. So far, she did seem responsive to me, but I just don't want to be yelling at her every night she decides to wake me up. I had one of my best friends coming over for dinner that night who possessed some strong psychic abilities, so maybe we'll all have a little pow-wow tonight.

While we were eating, I explained what was happening in the house with this girl. As I was trying to describe her, the name Anna popped into my head as well as an image of her with her long brown hair tied with a bow on each side. She was wearing a cream colored dress and white shoes with bows on the top. Her name was Anna. I didn't mention the image of her at all to my friend, Denise. I only told her that her name was Anna.

After dinner, we went into what from then on I called, "Anna's bedroom" and sat down on the couch to talk to her. We started asking who was the little girl in my house and we wanted to know why was she here. We intuitively got her name as Anna Elizabeth Marie and she was 8 years old. Her father had something to do with the building of the house and the top of the turret bedroom was her favorite place to be. She preferred staying in the house more than being with the rest of her family.

Denise was getting an image of what she looked like and without me mentioning anything about how I pictured Anna, she described her just as I saw her in my mind. Denise told me, "She has long light brown hair with a ribbon tied up on each side, a cream colored dress and dark brown lace up boots."

"Boots?" I asked. "I didn't see her wearing any boots." Denise replied, "Oh, she says she only wears the white shoes with the bows on top when she dresses up for you!" Well, I guess that explains it then!

Protective Anna.

I had lived in the house for seven years and had to deal with my little girl ghost constantly. I think she went into hiding during the renovation period. Maybe she didn't like all the noise. I think she loved having all the people over to the house on weekends. Every Sunday during the summer I'd have a barbecue and invite anyone who wanted to come over and join us. One Sunday Denise came over early to help out. It was a beautiful sunny afternoon and we estimated about 20 people would be showing up for dinner. I needed to run out to the store at the last minute, so I left her alone in the house, never thinking there might be an issue with Anna.

I had finished my errands and headed home. As I drove closer to the house, I could see Denise sitting out on the front lawn with a book and with Kitty curled up beside her. Kitty was our local beautiful outdoor cat that seemed to be owned by everyone on the street. For an outdoor cat, she was immaculately clean and white except for this little black mustache under her nose and a black stripe 'armband' around her front right leg. We all called her Kitty because that seemed to be the most obvious name and a name she actually responded to.

Most nights the cat would sleep on a small outdoor table and chair set right outside my bedroom. The chairs had cushions and Kitty loved to be curled up, positioning herself so she could see through my glass sliding doors and into my bedroom and watch me sleep. She was the best alarm clock. Every morning at 7:00 am she'd wake up and sit outside the door and "Meow!" that it was time for breakfast. I'd get out of bed and run down to the kitchen, but she'd always beat me there and be seated in the planter box outside the kitchen window. I'd love to have her in the house, but I am allergic to cats. Not anywhere near as bad as my brother or dad had, but if I started petting a cat within a few minutes, I'd start itching and sneezing.

There were always so many animals around the house since Griffith Park, the largest park in Los Angeles, was located just across the street. Lots of cute skunk and raccoon families with their babies, possums, deer and of course, coyotes. I've seen Kitty actually fight off a group of three small coyotes and escape. She was such a brave, smart cat. I am more attracted to dogs as a pet, but this cat was really special.

So, I pull into the driveway, park the car and walked over to see how Denise was doing. "Anna locked me out of the house!" she said. "I came outside to get my computer out of my car and when I tried to get back in, the front security gate had closed and locked," I told her that wasn't possible. The security gate had a metal latch that was tight and had to be manually flipped so the bolt would fall into place. It just wouldn't do that easily. She suggested I go look for myself.

I walked up to the front of the house and pulled on the door gate. It was locked. I thought I would enter the house from the main door and come back down to see how the door would have locked itself. I let myself in through the big door upstairs and came back downstairs to where my office was and the security gate. I looked at the latch and it was fully turned into the locked position from the inside.

"Anna! Why did you lock Denise outside? That was not very nice!" I said to my little ghost as I flipped the latch back to its open position. Denise entered through the door and I demonstrated how difficult it would be for a person to flip the lock, let alone a ghost! Once we got back upstairs we started preparing for the barbecue. My friend who we affectionately call, "Chef Paul" had arrived to begin preparing his world famous BBQ chicken.

As people started arriving and the prepared food was being set on the table, we noticed Denise had disappeared. We started asking if anyone had seen her, but no one had. I looked upstairs and then back down and out to the street where her car was parked, but no Denise. I even tried calling her cell phone, but it went straight to voicemail.

As the party increased in size, I decided to turn up the music in the living room. The controls for the music were inside a closet in the bathroom off the living room. I walked over and turned the handle and opened the door and found myself staring face to face with an angry Denise. "Don't tell me you didn't hear me yelling and banging on the door for the past half hour!" she cried. I tried to get her to calm down and told her that no one heard her and no one knew why she disappeared. "The door was locked and the doorknob would only spin and not catch to unlock and let me out!" she complained. I tried the doorknob myself and it worked fine. I showed her that when the knob is turned, the latch is released just as it should be.

"It must be Anna! She doesn't want me in the house and keeps locking me out!" she yelled. I must admit that did seem like a possibility, but why would she do something like that? We came to the conclusion that Anna was jealous of other women in the house and didn't want them around. She's such a possessive little ghost.

This idea continued when I had a friend of the family come out from Buffalo and stay with me for a few days. Jessica was 24, recently graduated from University of Buffalo and wanted to explore Southern California. I allowed her to stay in my master bedroom for greater privacy, while I settled into the guest room. My sleep patterns are pretty boring. I am usually in bed by 11, and am always up and having my morning coffee by 7. I am a good sleeper and only wake up occasionally when I have to pee, or when Anna is craving attention. While Jessica was visiting, I would let her sleep in and I would hear the shower turning on around 8:00 am. I'd be down on the first floor checking emails on my computer in the office by then and making our plans for the day.

On her second morning in the house, while I was still waiting for my coffee to kick in and staring at my computer screen, I heard Jessica screaming at the top of her lungs from the upstairs bathroom. I thought she must have fallen in the tub and broken her arm or leg by the intensity of the screaming. I jumped up from my desk and ran up the first flight of stairs to the living room landing. She continued screaming my name as I reached the bottom of the stairs leading to the 3rd floor. My heart was pounding in my chest as I looked up at the top of the stairs and saw her standing there wrapped in a towel, dripping wet. "You have to come see this! Come look in the bathroom!" she screamed.

I could see that she was walking ok, so that eliminated any thought of a broken leg. She also wasn't screaming in pain, so I assumed that meant her arms were ok, too. Now my thoughts were racing with a rush of adrenaline to imagine just what could have been so frightening in the bathroom. Maybe she found a spider. I live near a park with lots of trees around, so there are big spiders everywhere.

We turned the corner into the bedroom and I followed her into the bathroom. "Look!" she said. I looked around the bathroom and didn't see anything. "What am I looking for?" I asked. "The lights are ON!" she screamed.

I took notice and agreed with her that yes, indeed, the lights in the bathroom were on. Perhaps the lights were too bright for her. I asked her, "Is there something wrong with the lights?" She said no there wasn't anything wrong with the lights. She continued to explain that they were not on when she entered the tub. Once she was in the tub and showering, all the lights in the bathroom came on full, then dimmed to off and came back up again and repeated turning on and off until she started screaming. The instant we both ran back into the bathroom, the lights just stayed on.

I have two separate dimmer switches in the bathroom. The main ceiling light is controlled by a dimmer on the wall where you would enter the bathroom. Facing you is a countertop with two sinks and two mirrors. There is another switch on the far wall by the sink to the right that controls the lights over the mirrors. These switches are completely separate from each other and it would be very difficult to have them both sliding on and off at the same time.

I confirmed with Jessica one more time, "Are you sure you didn't have the lights on when you got into the tub?"

"I am absolutely certain that all the lights in the bathroom were off when I went to shower. There is plenty of morning light in here and I didn't need to have any of the lights on!" she defended herself.

I had told her about Anna being in the house even before Jessica had arrived, so I tried to make her feel better by saying, "Maybe that was Anna's way of welcoming you to California!" Anna can be so thoughtful.

Over the next four days while Jess was here we had planned a full itinerary of all the tourist sights in SoCal, including Disneyland, Universal Studios, and the beaches, so maybe with all the day's distractions, she forgot about Anna and the Magical Bathroom Lighting experience.

I slept well that night and woke up as I usually do. I grabbed my coffee and headed down to my office since there was no screaming emanating from the upstairs bathroom. Of course, the same thing wouldn't happen again. That would be too predictable and Anna is more creative than that. Then again, maybe Anna enjoyed listening to Jessica scream because just as sat down my mug of coffee, there she was yelling at the top of her lungs again. "Rick, HURRY! Come upstairs NOW!" she yelled.

At least this time I knew what to expect. I flew up both sets of stairs and ran into the bathroom to see if I could catch the light show. Jessica was standing in the middle of the bathroom wrapped in a towel and pointing to the ceiling lights. "She did it again! She was playing with the lights again, turning them up and down, but this time really fast. Up and down. As soon as you stepped into the bedroom, the lights just stayed on!" she explained.

So if Anna wasn't welcoming Jessica to California, maybe she was trying to scare her into going back home. "Anna! This is no way to treat my houseguest! She is only going to be here for two more days, so please try to be nice, ok?" I suggested. Jessica didn't seem as scared the second time and even thought to ask me if the lights had ever done that before. I told her I've showered and taken jacuzzi baths in here many times and never had an issue with the lights. It was a special show just for her.

Jessica's last two days were filled with tours and shows around Los Angeles, but the next morning I wasn't downstairs on the computer. This time I would be ready for Anna by waiting in the guest room so I could hear if anything happens while Jessica was in the shower this morning. I felt like a stalker, waiting for my victim to enter the shower. I stood quietly, sipping my coffee and heard the water come on in the master bathroom. After only a few minutes, I heard Jessica loudly whisper my name, "Rick! Come in now!"

I set my coffee down, ran into the bedroom and quickly turned into the bathroom and saw the lights on again with Jessica in a towel. "What did I miss now?" I asked.

"It was different this time!" she said. "Anna turned on the lights over the mirrors, but they were going on and off separately!"

I told her, "That's not possible. Both of those lights are on the same switch. They can't go on and off independently." I walked over and pressed the dimmer switch to off and the lights turned off. I raised the dimmer and they both come back on again.

Jessica said, "That's not what they just did. When the left one was on, the right one was off and then they'd switch!"

I thought that was fascinating and told Anna, "Anna! You never told me you were an electrician! You could have saved me hundreds of dollars in renovations, clever girl!"

We went out and had another fun day touring around the city, had a nice dinner and slept well that night. The next morning was Jessica's last day staying with me and instead of hearing screams, I only heard the quiet sound of running water. No light show. Maybe Anna couldn't come up with any more lighting configurations, so she decided not to do anything, or maybe she knew Jessica was leaving! Jessica returned that afternoon to Buffalo with not only lots of travel pics but a very nice story to tell everyone about my little ghost, Anna. Thank you, Anna.

House for sale.

The renovation had taken too long and by the time I was ready to sell, it was late 2008, the beginning of the real estate crash. I had an appraisal on the property for $2M, but we started low at $1.8M thinking that would stir up some activity. There was talk about the real estate market decline, but I never thought that would be a problem in this very desirable area of Los Feliz.

We had so many people come through the house and held an open house every weekend. We lowered the price twice and each time even more prospective buyers wandered through. Everybody loved the house, admired my art collection, but no offers. Something wasn't right. I had begun doing energy clearings for clients because I know what happens when people's energy gets stuck.

Energy attracts energy and we end up dumping all this energy into our living space where the accumulation of other people's energy can drain us, cause confusion, and even deliver physical pain. I would clear out all the stuck energy in their home and use them to bring their own clear energy back into their space. This allows for an increase in energy, creativity, and clarity, along with the alleviation of any stress and associated pain.

I was living in the house and close to Anna and her energy. If people were coming in and feeling that the energy in the house was off, then I needed to do an energy clearing on my own house. Denise came over and we sat down to find out what was going on. We needed to have a discussion with Anna. Anna admitted that she was jealous of having Denise around. That's why she locked her outside and in the bathroom. Anna also didn't want me to move. She made the upstairs portion of the house uncomfortable for any prospective buyers so no offers were made.

We gave her an option. Either she participates and helps in the sale of the house or I would be reconnecting her to her family and she would have to go and be with them. Anna agreed to help so she could stay in the house. She would eventually be reconnected with her family, but she still liked hanging out here with me. I did a clearing on the house and with Anna's new attitude towards selling, we would wait and see if anything changed.

The following Sunday we almost decided to cancel the open house because of this terrible heat wave that had set upon the city of Los Angeles. It was going to be over 110 degrees that day and both of my realtors and I thought no one would show. We had a call from a couple that really wanted to see the house, so we decided to go ahead and hold it open. What made the heat worse was the fact that there was no breeze. No air was circulating. The trees around the house weren't moving, just hanging in the dry heat. I closed all the doors and windows, put out some bottled waters and cranked up the a/c. It was later, around 3:00 pm when they finally showed up. They seemed to be a very nice couple, but obviously a bit weary after seeing several other homes before mine.

My realtors, Tony and Linda, were a great team. In larger homes, one realtor could be showing the property while the other was positioned as greeter so no one has to walk into an empty house. The couple had entered through the main door in the living room and Tony was escorting them upstairs. I was still in the living room with Linda when suddenly, the very large, heavy main entry door closed with a loud "SLAM!" Linda jumped and said, "What the hell was that?" I looked over at the now closed door and said, "That was our little Anna closing the door to help keep the cool air inside." Linda was still not used to all the ghost talk in the house and said, "She did not do that! It must have been the wind."

We were standing less than 10 feet from the door when it closed and I told Linda to go open the door for me. She walked over to the door, pressed the latch and started to pull the door open. The door was not only about 7 feet high, it was over 4 feet wide and 2 inches thick. This heavy door opens over a thick entry carpet and had to be pulled with great effort. Linda started laughing and said, "I had no idea this door was so difficult to open!"

I asked her to step outside and feel the nice breeze. She replied, "What breeze? There's no breeze out here. There's hardly any air at all, it's so hot!"

I turned to her and said, "Linda, that is exactly my point. There was no wind to blow the door closed and now you see just how difficult that would have been with the size of the door and the drag on the carpet. Remember, Anna promised to help sell the house now, so her way of assisting was to make sure the front door was closed to help keep the place cool!"

Linda said, "Stop! You're freaking me out. Where is she now?" I told her she was sitting over on the chaise lounge, not far from the front door. Linda started to look a little worried. "Don't worry. You'll be fine. She doesn't bite!" I said with a smile. I apologized for Anna later and explained that she really is a very sweet eight-year-old girl who happens to be a spirit. I told Linda, "You shouldn't hold that against her. It's not her fault!"

The price of the house was still coming down and I thought having new realtors might help. One night before bed, I did an energy clearing on the house. I burned my favorite combination of salts, herbs, and alcohol in a pan and walked it through each floor. I was stressing as I went to bed and finally had a heart to heart with my three spirit guides, Luke, Noah, and Abe. I told them I tried everything I thought I could do to sell or rent this house and this crash was taking its toll not only on me but on some of the neighbor's properties as well. I'm surrendering. Before bed, I told my spirit guides, "You guys know more than I do, so I'm sure you'll come up with a better solution for me. I give up. I'm leaving it up to you, now. Thank you, I love you and good night!" Then I rolled over and went to sleep.

The next day was outstanding. My realtor called me first thing in the morning and told me we had an offer. It was low, but I had time to make a counter-offer. When my realtor called again in the afternoon, I was not ready to make a decision. He told me I didn't have to. We just received a second offer at a higher price. I was so full of gratitude that I was about to explode. I was yelling through the house, "I have the best guides in the world!"...

Later that day I received my 3rd offer on the house. It was hand written with drawings of cats all over it. My realtors never took it seriously, so they never responded. A few weeks later, after both offers fell out, I was having a garage sale out on my driveway. It is amazing how much stuff we can accumulate in just a few years. I was encouraged to sell whatever I could, that way I would have less to move.

It was mid-afternoon on Sunday when an SUV pulled up to the front of the house. A woman got out of the driver side of the car and walked over to me. She introduced herself and asked if the house was still for sale. When I told her that it was, she said she had her client in the car with her. They just happened to be driving by as they were looking at open houses in the area.

"Why didn't you respond to our offer?" she asked. I had to take a step back and think about the question for a second. I assured her that my realtors and I responded to every offer we received on the house. She reached into her shoulder bag and pulled out the offer that was handwritten and had cats all over it. I had to explain to her that I did see that offer, but that my realtors did not take it seriously because no one hand writes offers anymore. "Well, my client thought it would be a special touch because she and her husband really love your house" she affirmed. I apologized and told them we'd get back to them this evening about the offer.

As it turned out, this was the couple that finally bought my castle. We had a signed agreement and I began packing things up, starting first in the bedroom. As I was assembling a box for my extensive thirsty towel collection, I heard the front doorbell ring. This is one of those new wireless bells that has a battery inside the signal depressor that attaches to the outside of the door. The box that contains the bell is inserted into any normal outlet and will ring with a variety of chimes when signaled. This time someone was outside and constantly ringing the bell, driving me crazy.

I ran down the stairs and pulled the door open and there was no one there. The bell continued to ring so I unhooked the device and pulled out the battery to make it stop. There was no one on the stairway or in the driveway, so I ran down to the street. There was no one there either. I marched back in the house to have a word with Anna. "Ohhhhh. I get it. You're excited for me that the house has finally sold, so you decided to lean on my doorbell. That's cute. Ok, then. Thank you, Anna!" I said as I put the battery back inside the case and reattached it to the doorframe.

She continued with the doorbell game two more times that night and several times the next day until I just decided to remove the doorbell entirely from the front door and remove the battery. If someone wants my attention, they can knock! I was just inside packing boxes anyway.

I still had no idea where I was going to move to, but I had ninety days to find a place. I was very concerned about Kitty. She wouldn't be happy being confined to apartment living after having the freedom of a large park at her disposal. The neighbors would still be there for her to feed and take care of her, but I would miss her terribly. I had grown very fond of that cat, and so had Anna.

It was about 7:30 on a Friday night when I heard someone knocking on the downstairs door. I opened the door to see my neighbor from down the street. He asked me, "Don't you own that white cat that runs around the neighborhood?"

I said, "She is more of a community cat in the area with lots of owners. Why?" I noticed he was swaying a bit and with the next breeze, I got a whiff of alcohol on him.

He took a deep breath and said, "I am sorry to tell you, but I just found her in the road, lying there. You know how fast these kids drive up and down this street. One of them must have hit her. When I got out of my truck to see if she was ok, she was already dead."

I was in shock. I told him, "That is not possible. She's incredibly fast and besides that, she's white! Even on a dark street, you can't miss her. Are you sure it's the same cat?"

He swayed again and answered, "Yes, the same white cat with the little black mustache. I know how you must feel. I have animals myself, so I will take care of it and bury her behind my house next to some of our animals that have died." He had a pet cemetery behind his house? This was already sounding too creepy and I wanted this conversation to end.

I told him, "That would be very nice. Thank you for letting me know and have a good night." He wished me a good night in return and staggered down the driveway.

I still to this day think he was the one who ran over Kitty. It was early on a Friday night and he had a few drinks and was in a hurry to get home. Not paying attention to the road, and Kitty probably thinking this truck will stop for me because I'm cute, he ran right over her. Guilt brought him to my door. I closed the door and sat down on the couch and wondered if this could be true. This was one really smart cat and I just found it hard to believe she could be killed by a truck. Coyotes maybe, but a truck you can see coming. It has headlights. I turned on the TV and tried to watch something. Anything. I needed to get my mind off of the possibility that Kitty was dead.

Then it began. I think anyone else would have run out of the house as fast as they could, but I was used to strange things happening in houses and I always try to rationalize every situation. Two hours had passed and I was still staring blindly at the TV when BAM! The house shook. Someone downstairs had forcefully slammed one of the doors and probably broke it off its hinges. I ran downstairs to take a look and turned on all the lights. All the doors were open. There was a door to the laundry room, one to the bathroom and one to my office. I saw no one down here, nothing broken and everything was where it should be. I switched the lights off and went back to my TV watching, with my heart still pounding in my chest.

After just thirty minutes had passed, I heard another BAM! just as loud as the first one, but coming from one of the upstairs bedrooms instead. It must have been Anna's room. I ran upstairs to check and found all the doors still wide open and no damage was done considering the force of the slam. Still confused, I walked once again back to the couch and sat down. By this time I had no idea what I was even watching. I was just waiting patiently to see if it was going to happen again.

And it did. Only 15 minutes later another BAM! from downstairs again with me running there fast to see if I could see anything. Not fast enough because all was fine. The slamming went on for another hour and I had to do something to make it stop. Something had pissed Anna off and she was taking it out on the house. Kitty! She must have found out that the cat was dead! I yelled to her, "Anna! I know you're upset. So am I. I did not kill the cat. It was our neighbor down the street. I think you should take out your frustrations on him and not on me. If you break anything I'm not going to fix it and the whole house will fall down, so please STOP!" There were a few seconds of silence before the final blast. I was still sitting on the couch when 23 feet up on the roof, in the center of the ceiling over the living room, was one final enormous BOOM! shaking the whole house. She seemed to be done for now but was obviously terribly upset over the cat.

As I went to bed that night, I looked outside through my bedroom window to the seat cushion that

Kitty occupied every night. I was hoping that maybe the wrong cat had been hit and that Kitty was fine and would be sitting out there waiting for me to climb into bed. Even as I switched off the reading light by my bed, there was only an empty cushion outside.

When I woke up the next morning still seeing no cat, it started to really hit me that the cat was gone. I was surprised how emotional I became over the next week, not realizing how attached I was to that animal. Every Sunday morning I would take my coffee and my bowl of oatmeal out to the balcony and sit under my umbrella reading the LA Times. Kitty would be curled up alongside me while we would be observing all the morning activity in the park. Every time I thought of her, I got a lump in my throat. It helped me realize that it was really time to move on.

We had several inspections and I became very familiar with the new owners. They had just sold a smaller house over on Beachwood Canyon. I just assumed if they lived on that canyon street, one of the oldest in Hollywood, that they would for sure have lots of ghost stories for me. That was the street that would take you up to the old "Hollywoodland" sign built in 1923 for the Hollywoodland real estate development company that served the area. The sign had many ghost sightings from failed actors and actresses who jumped from the sign to their death. The old castle-like houses on the street were full of ghost stories and if that wasn't enough, one of the most famous houses on the street was the Westshire Manor, or Castle La Paloma or just simply known as the Bela Lugosi house!

During the inspections, my realtors insisted that I not mention anything about Anna. "You never know how people are going to take that. Some people could freak out and walk away," they told me. "But these guys are different!" I would say, defending them. "I'm sure their old house must have had at least one ghost. What if they ask me if it's haunted?" I pleaded. "No!" they firmly replied. I continued through the inspections and kept my mouth shut.

The house finally closed to the joy of the new couple receiving it and I felt it was taking a piece of me with it. I had put so much of myself into that house and at the same time, I experienced a great spiritual growth and education through Anna. She may have been very angry that Kitty was dead, but in her place, the new owners brought with them four big house cats. I often wondered why the new owners never called me about noises inside the house and then I realized they could always blame it on the cats.

About four months after the close of escrow, I was invited back over to see some of the improvements they had done on the house. Owning a house is like having a child. It always needs something. I drove over expecting to see a whole new house but actually, the house looked and felt much as it did when I lived there. They put in new hard wood floors throughout the upstairs and stairway. No more creaking stairs. That was always another built in alarm system for me. You could never walk up those stairs at night without waking me up unless you were a ghost!

They had covered the furniture with large white sheets to prevent any construction dust from getting on it. As they were showing me around, I saw some cool gargoyle lighting sconces, which I liked, and make the house feel even more like a castle. Anna's room up on top of the 3rd floor was now the husband's office, while my office on the first floor became a big cat bed where all four cats made themselves home.

These cats were all big and each with its own personality. Three were all about the same size and very friendly. The largest of them all was this enormous black cat that seemed like if he stretched out, would be at least four feet long. His name was Merlin and he very rarely came out of his room, which was just fine for me with my allergies.

They served a deliciously healthy lunch and we talked about their work and future plans for the house. I still felt I could not volunteer any information about Anna. I was waiting for them to say something about ghosts, or just give me a clue that you might have seen something in the house. Nothing. Maybe Anna decided to join her family after all.

We finished lunch, walked through the living room and I stood by the end of the long, covered couch. As we were talking, the cats were roaming around observing us when suddenly a large black face peered around the bottom of the stairs. Merlin! He slowly rounded the corner until I could fully see the true length of this large cat. His owners stood quietly by in awe as he glided across the floor and jumped onto the arm of the covered sofa.

It seems he had a plan or was on a mission. With perfect balance, he placed one paw in front of the other and walked over to where I standing. I make it a point not to pet cats because I'll start itching and sneezing, so I just looked down into his big green eyes. He lifted a paw and placed it on my stomach while the other reached up and landed on my chest. He raised his body up with both paws on my chest now and stared into my eyes. His head was moving closer to my face and I could hear Lisa make an audible gasp as we almost ended up nose to nose. Apparently, this was not normal behavior for this cat. So I would not startle him, I slowly lifted my hand and started to run my hand down his back. I could feel the vibration of his purring and realized this great big guy just wanted to come over and say hello.

Lisa and Steeg had never seen their cat do anything like that before but seemed glad we made a connection. I've always had an affinity for animals and they would always seem comfortable around me. I was wondering if this was Merlin's way of telling me that he knows about the cat that was here before they all showed up and that Kitty was ok. He had made such a definitive statement by his presence that I have to believe it was for something more than just a casual hello.

Until I could find another haunted renovation, I rented an apartment on Sunset Blvd in Hollywood and would drive by my old house whenever I was in the neighborhood to see how it looked and how my trees were doing. Exactly one year to the date the house sold, I received a text from Lisa saying, "Rick, why didn't you tell me the house was haunted?"

"Lisa," I replied, "You never asked me!"

With each and every encounter, I was learning so much. I have always been aware of energies, spirits, and entities, but now I was discovering that I could enjoy their company. My biggest and most frightening lesson was yet to come, which I would have never expected because I was living in a new building that had no history of ghosts. I learned ghosts are not stuck to the place they died. They are all looking for a place where they belong.

Chapter 9

GHOST TOURS IN QUEBEC CITY

2010

Everything was manageable to a point until I got to Montréal. I sold my little haunted castle the year before and took advantage of a special deal offered by JetBlue Airlines. You could fly anywhere that JetBlue flew for the entire month of September for only $699. I flew to 15 cities in 30 days. It was an amazing vacation and probably one of the best I ever had. The two places that I personally wanted to explore were Québec City and the coast of Maine. I decided to explore Quebec City first. Since JetBlue does not fly to Canada, I had to fly to Bloomington, Vermont, rent a car and drive up to meet my friend Claude in Montréal.

Claude was a wonderful friend who visited me many times in Los Angeles and I even had the opportunity to introduce him to Anna while he stayed with me. This was my first time visiting him on his turf. I spent one day touring about Montréal, slept in a wonderful old B&B and then we left for Québec City the next morning. It was a beautiful drive and gave us an opportunity to catch up. We stayed in a hotel that resembled an old castle or fort, drank lots of coffee and had an amazing dinner in the old section of Québec City.

After dinner, we did something special. We signed up for the "Ghost Tours of Québec". I thought this could be a tax deduction since it was my job to talk to ghosts anyway! At 10:00 pm we were greeted by a man in historical garb carrying an old lantern. He was wearing a trench coat and a large old hat and was giving a commentary about some basic information we needed to know before we began our tour. He emphasized the importance of sticking together along our tour route since it was dark and getting lost would have been very easy.

As our group began slowly walking out of the courtyard, he started telling us all about the history of Montréal. We crossed over the bridge and he pointed out that 300 years ago a boat had sunk here. He mentioned that more people had drowned in this incident than on the Titanic! We also went to sections of the city where people were shot, beheaded, murdered, etc. but no real mention of any ghosts.

Our last stop was a beautiful old church. As he led us inside, he failed to turn on any of the lights. We all stood there in this dark church while he told us another story. There was nothing particularly scary or alarming about the story. I was more interested in seeing the architecture of the church and didn't understand why we were standing there in the dark.

When the tour was over we all said goodbye outside the church. As everyone was leaving I lingered so I would be able to ask our tour guide a few questions. "Why was there no mention of ghosts along the advertised Ghost Tour that you just gave us?" I asked. "If you really want to know the answer, it is because most of our ghost stories are inside the local hotels. If we divulge any of that information, we can get lawsuits from those hotels complaining that we are telling stories that could affect their business," he answered. I told him I usually get a feeling if there are any ghosts around, but said that I honestly never felt anything along the entire tour. He explained, "Yes, I'm sorry about that. It really is more of a 'This is Where a Lot of People Died' Tour!" I thanked him for his candor and his time. We said good night and continued our walk back to the hotel for the night.

The next morning, Claude and I went and had breakfast in town. We took a scenic walk back to the hotel and along the way passed a wonderful series of old row houses along a hillside. At the top of the hill, standing all by itself, was an amazing home built in the mid-1850s. Standing there in front of the house, I looked over to Claude and asked him if he could see the old man in the upstairs window. He said he didn't see anyone. I told him that there was this gaunt, old man shaking his finger at us, trying to get our attention.

Then within a matter of 10 or 15 seconds, I was imparted with so much information, that I was not able to verbally keep up with everything I was learning in that short period of time. Physically, I noticed that my heart was racing very fast and that every hair on my body was standing on end from my feet to the tops of my ears.

I started telling him about this man and his life in the house. He had lived there a very long time and had seen his family come and go. Right now, I could sense that he was feeling very lonely and desperately wanted someone to keep him company in this big house. He loved having his family and friends in the house and enjoyed having people around him all the time. His favorite memory was when his son had turned the downstairs of the house into a restaurant. This made him so happy to have all these wonderful people come into the house for friendly conversation and a meal. Then something happened to one of the family members and they had to close the restaurant. I was getting a rush of emotion and information and trying to piece together everything I was feeling about the history of this incredible man.

Over the years, as the family members were had died off, someone close to him was buried in the ground behind the house. The man was very disturbed that someone built a brick extension off the back of the house, covering up the gravesite of where the family member was buried. The house was in good shape and seemed to be withstanding the weathering storms and intense Canadian cold. Someone was taking good care of this home.

The man seemed so excited and pleased to find someone who could finally listen and understand all he had to say. My initial thought was if I'm in Québec City where the main language is French, wouldn't he be communicating to me in French? How am I able to understand all the information I have been receiving? I became aware of the fact that an energetic conversation is an intuitive transfer of information and doesn't really have a language. I am receiving feelings and emotions and thoughts and then I translate all of that into words, as best I can.

Claude and I walked slowly up the steps of the front porch. We cupped our hands over our eyes and peered in through the front window. The sun was shining brightly on this cold, crisp September morning, providing us with enough light to see inside. There were no boards covering the windows of the vacant house and with the strong light gleaming through the dusty glass, we could clearly see what was once a restaurant. The living room was full of small tables with wooden chairs placed upside down on the tabletops. We could also see how they converted the living room to be able to accommodate people who were dining there. Right by the front door stood the old menu board with tripod legs that they would put out on the street so people walking by could see what the restaurant had to offer that night.

We walked back down the front steps and toured around the side of the house, looking in the windows, continuing on to the back of the house where we stopped. There in front of us, clearly as the old man had described earlier, was the brick addition to the home. The odd thing about this addition was that there were no doors or windows that we could see. It was such a strange thing to add onto a house and we could only assume it served as a food and supply storage for the restaurant.

All the time we are walking I am also hearing and feeling the man inside the house. He has been in the house alone for some time now. He says he feels that the house has been on the market for a long time and he is concerned about finding the right people to purchase his beautiful home. As of now, there have been no homebuyers that he wanted to share his house with.

Claude and I were still planning on leaving that morning to drive back to Montréal. I waved goodbye to our new friend and we started to head towards the hotel. After traveling a block or so, I mentioned to

Claude that our friend was still with me and my heart was still racing. This man was still so excited to have someone to share his thoughts and feelings with, he didn't want us to go. I actually felt him on my shoulders, like I was now carrying him with me. Claude wanted to stop for some coffee on the corner. I said to our nice, ghostly friend, "Stop, please!" I said. "Where do you think you're going?"

My heart was pounding in my chest now and I had goose bumps all over my arms and my legs from his energy. I stopped on the street and told Claude that I need to have a conversation with this man. I spoke directly to him, "I appreciate the fact that you shared all this wonderful information with me, but I am not the one you are waiting for. You cannot come with me. You must go back inside your house because that is where you need to be now. I can assure you that a nice family is coming along very soon that will also hear you and they are the ones that will purchase your house and take care of it. I am just here to give you that message."

At that moment it felt like he just jumped off my shoulders. I stood there for a minute or two thinking about what just happened. The odd sensation in my shoulders and back was gone and I even felt lighter now. We continued walking up to the top of the hill and before ducking inside a coffee shop, I turned and waved goodbye to my French friend and wished him luck. Claude and I finished our coffee, checked out of the hotel and had a great time discussing our "Ghost Tour" of Quebec City on the drive back to Montreal.

Each of my experiences was increasing my awareness and expanding my knowledge of this amazing unseen world. Looking back on the situation now, I could have asked him if there were any family members that he would have liked to reconnect with, but I wouldn't learn this option until later. For now, he seemed to be content in his home with his memories until a new family came along. The fact that he attached himself onto my shoulders was also something I was not terribly comfortable with. I'm sure there must be repercussions from something like that, as I was soon to find out.

Chapter 10

JONATHAN'S GHOST

2012

As my client list was growing for my energy clearings, I started getting requests for something else. People were sensing something in their homes that wasn't just stuck energy. There was something heavier and darker turning up. I was remembering what the other spiritualists and psychics had told me years ago. "Be careful in pursuing ghosts. You don't know what you're getting into," they would tell me. Of course, I don't know what I'm getting into. That's because no one would tell me anything. I felt like if they were to actually say what it was I was supposed to fear, then that would manifest the fear and make it a reality.

I am an eternal optimist and never felt anything dark or evil, or maybe those entities were just avoiding me. I already survived a near death experience and if I was supposed to leave this human existence, it would have happened right then. I had so many close calls and I'm still here to tell about them, so I maybe my job here is not done yet. Maybe there's something more I have to do. This is where I finally had the opportunity to see and experience exactly what they were warning me about.

Denise was here from New York City just after Hurricane Sandy had forced her to relocate from her apartment building by the South Street Seaport. The building had been condemned due to gas leaks and no one was allowed back in until the situation could be rectified, which could take months. When the tenants left their apartments, they were not allowed to go back inside under any circumstances. Whatever you brought out of the building with you after the first evacuation, was all you had. Denise at least had left with her computer, a purse stuffed with a few extra pair of underwear, a jacket, and what she was wearing at the time. She bought a plane ticket to LA and went to stay in a building her parents managed in Hollywood.

Her mom brought her into an empty two bedroom that was vacant and told her she could stay there. She rented a car and headed to Costco to get all of the immediate necessities, like an air mattress, dishes, a printer, and food. She called me often within the first four days of setting up her new temporary home. The message was always the same. "Rick, I don't know what's happening here. I am incredibly depressed. I've never felt this way before and I don't know where it's coming from," she'd tell me.

I would try to comfort her each time by telling reminding her, "Look at what you just went through! That hurricane was devastating and you could have lost everything you owned. At least there's hope knowing that you can eventually go back to your apartment and continue your life there. That's something to look forward to. Just breathe and be grateful that you have a safe place to be right now."

She tried to be away from the apartment building as much as possible. Keeping busy and then coming back at the end of a long day and just wanting to sleep was a good way of ignoring any depression. After a few months of this, she finally received a message that her building was once again safe to enter and she could now return home.

I came over to help her get organized for her trip back to New York. We returned some of the things she never had a chance to use and then went out for a nice dinner. We headed back to the apartment she had been living in for the past few months. This was my first time seeing her temporary place. Her things were scattered around the room, half packed. I knelt down by the bedroom door and started picking up some loose items that needed to be boxed. I was by the door and gave it a push with my hand. The door swung open and then swung back. I pushed it again, and again, it came back. I stood up to see what was going on with the door, pushed it fully open and walked inside.

I instantly felt every hair on my body stand on end and at the same time, felt an overwhelming sadness come over me. I yelled out to Denise, "What is going on in this room? There is definitely something in here!"

She yelled back, "I tried to tell you, but you weren't listening to me. I wasn't depressed from the hurricane. I was depressed from something in the apartment!"

Ok, I get it now. "You should have been more specific when you were explaining how you felt," I assured her. "How did you ever sleep in here?" I asked.

She said, "It's not really in the bedroom. More like in the closet, so I just kept the door closed!"

I opened that closet door and felt the ghost of a terrified 7-year-old boy hiding there. I asked him if he was ok. He told me his name was Jonathan and that he was too scared to leave the closet and refused to come out. Denise asked, "Who are you talking to?"

"His name is Jonathan. He's 7-years-old and said he is too scared to come out. He won't tell me why, but he feels very safe in your closet!" I answered.

She continued to yell from the other room, "Tell him there's a school right across the street. I'm sure there's a lot of dead kids he could go play with over there!" I'm sure that wasn't the answer Jonathan was looking for. I could feel how scared he was and I thought the best thing for him would be to connect him with a family member who has already crossed over. I would try to find him someone who could take him to where he was supposed to be.

I asked Jonathan if he had any brothers or sisters over there that he'd like to see. He told me both his brother and sister were older than him and always picked on him and he didn't want to see them. "How about your father, then? Would you like to see him?" I asked. Jonathan didn't care to see him either. I tried one last person, "Ok then. How about your mother?"

"Yes! I want to see my Mom!" he confessed.

At least now I had an idea of how to help him. My youngest guide is great at locating other spirit energies, so I sent Luke to go find Jonathan's mother. Energetic connections are instantaneous and there is no sense of time as we know it in the spirit world. When Luke returned with Jonathan's mother, his whole being lit up. I never got the story of how he was separated from his family, but he seemed very happy to be going back. When I reconnect spirits to wherever they are supposed to be, I always tell them, "Please, don't contact or touch any humans directly, because it connects us to your energies and emotions, giving us confusion and pain. Go with love and light and be happy!"

153

Denise was standing by my side now as Jonathan waved goodbye to me. As they both left, we felt a cool breeze in the room and I could feel Jonathan's relief, joy, and excitement about returning to his family. The room seemed lighter now and I'm sure she would have no trouble sleeping in here tonight. She thanked me, gave me hug and I left to drive back home.

Doing energy work can be exhausting and you must remember to protect your own energy in the process. I was so tired when I got home I had just enough energy to shower, throw on my favorite night shirt and jump into bed. As I reached to turn off the light by my bed, I felt something in the room. Something heavy was making it almost hard to breathe. My head hit the pillow and I thought I was just overly tired and needed to sleep. The air was thick and I knew something wasn't right.

When I opened my eyes, I realized at that moment what Jonathan was terrified of and why he would not leave the protection of his closet. There was a man standing at the foot of my bed. Surrounding him was a mound of depression from the ground up to his thighs. This was the guy Jonathan was trying to avoid and now I understood why.

"No! No! No! I am not going to deal with you tonight. I am very sorry, but you have to go. I need to sleep and you have too much baggage for me to deal

154

with you tonight. Please leave!" and at that, I put my head down and fell asleep.

There is a magic hour when our guides want to talk to us or have something important they want us to know. It is at 3:30 am. If you are sound asleep and suddenly wake up for no reason at all, take a look at the clock and check the time. Chances are it will be very close to 3:30. Make sure there was nothing else around that woke you and then listen to your intuition and see if there is any conversation there. Don't look for anything with your eyes and don't listen with your ears. Sense how you feel at this moment, listen to your breathing and see what happens.

I woke up exactly at 3:30 am, but this was no message from my guides. I was in extreme pain. As I attempted to open my eyes, my head felt like it was going to explode. I rarely get headaches, but this was the worst migraine I have ever had. It felt like my head was put in a vice, but not only from the front to the back but also both sides as well as the top of my head. I tried to see if anything fell on my head while I was sleeping and found nothing. As I turned my head and tried to sit up, I felt a shooting pain along my spine, up from my back through to my neck and made it extremely difficult to move. I slowly reached over and turned on the light, but the light hurt my eyes, so I quickly shut it off again. I felt this pain was too great to ignore, so I made my way to the bathroom to grab some Advil and swallowed four of them hoping for immediate relief.

I assumed I must have hurt my back at the gym and pinched a nerve in my neck. My mind was racing and trying to find any clue at all what might be causing this physical state of intense pain and discomfort. I splashed some cold water on my face, dried off with a towel and staggered back into bed. I know my body very well and I normally would choose a holistic or Chinese form of pain relief and therapy before any local doctors. As I was waiting for the aspirin to work I was thinking if I was able to drive later, I would try to get acupuncture and see if increasing my circulation would help. Maybe a massage or a chiropractic visit if something was actually pinched. How did I do this to myself?

The pain did not lessen. I'd fall asleep for a while, wake up and roll over to see if a different position would help. I woke up later sweating, thinking the aspirin was supposed to help with fevers, so why am I sweating? I was getting concerned that I might have to somehow drag myself to the emergency room at Cedar's hospital because I cannot pinpoint exactly what is happening to me and there has been no sign of improvement.

I wanted to give this a little more time to see what would happen and I thought a cup of coffee might help. I had some work that I needed to do on my computer, but when I tried to focus on the screen, it was a complete blur and I was unable to see anything to get any work done. The coffee was not helping plus this heavy feeling in my apartment was still there and was making me feel extremely isolated and depressed.

What if I can't work and something was seriously wrong with me? I've been spoiled my entire life by excellent health, never been on any medications, never having ever been diagnosed with anything outside of a cold and even surviving a bad motorcycle accident. At three separate times that day I thought I would just lie down for a minute and each time I slept for over an hour. I need to get outside. I need some fresh air.

I walked down to my bank, just a few blocks down from my building. The bright afternoon sun still hurt my eyes and my head even with sunglasses on, but I made it to the bank and deposited my checks. On the way back something happened.

At first, I thought I was having a moment of clarity where I could see things as they really are. I could see my apartment building in the distance and realized how organized and in order my life was. I downsized after selling my big house and was able to sell off all of my excess furniture and art from two large storage units with a feeling of great achievement. Everything I owned, along with and all of my important documents, were all in my apartment and easily accessible. I was feeling like my job here was done. I had a wonderful life filled with great opportunities and experiences and now I am very curious to see what happens after we lose our carbon exteriors and cross over to our spiritual selves once again. It has to be very easy. We just let go, right? Well, here's my chance.

Everything was happening as if I was watching a movie. The bus that had stopped on Sunset and Fairfax and picked up a few riders was now barreling down the street towards me. All I would have to do was take three steps to my right and I would be in the direct path of the oncoming bus. Since everything I own is in order and my life is complete, now is the perfect time to explore the other side. In just a few seconds it would all be over and I'd get to experience first hand what it would be like to transition, to see how it all happens and have instant answers to all of life's unanswered questions.

I started justifying how and why I should die today. It was all too easy and I paused for a second to see where this voice was coming from. This was not a conversation I would ever have because I have never been depressed a day in my life and never experienced a thought of suicide. I would often suggest to my doctors that I have too much serotonin in my brain, and I'm always too happy. If there was a way to pull some out and start sharing it, I gladly would. This voice of depression was just not me. It was not what I call my authentic voice. If it wasn't me, then who was it?

I stood on the street, pulled out my phone and texted Denise, who was safely back in New York City by now. No answer. I texted Lynn, another psychic I know in Santa Monica and I sent her a message that I was having a problem. I told her that I felt like something attached to me while I was doing a clearing at Denise's the night before. What she texted back made my heart stop. Lynn said, "Be very careful. They will try to talk you into suicide." How did she know that? That was amazingly right on. Did everyone know this except me and why had no one told me about this before? I think I was discovering that warning that everyone was telling me about, but no one ever explained to me. What was I supposed to do now?

Lynn told me she had a friend who wrote a book about this and she would find out from her what I should do and get back to me. I continued walking back to my apartment and when I got inside, I sat down to self-examine how I was feeling. I had the same body aches, back and neck pain and the pressing migraine. This feeling of sadness and despair was still hanging on me and couldn't concentrate on anything except finding a way out.

I finally heard back from Lynn and she said she was able to contact her friend who emailed me a page with a paragraph I should recite to clear the bad energy away. I thanked her for her help and went to my computer. I read through the page in the email and located the section that was to be read aloud. It began, "Any energy or entity that is not supposed to be here, needs to leave now…"

I believe everyone has their own special talents and abilities along with their own unique ways of achieving resolutions. I can see where this would come in handy and be effective for clearing things away that you cannot see, but the man standing in his own mound of depression was once again standing right in front of me. I decided to do what it is I do best. Talk to him directly.

I did the same thing I did with Jonathan. I asked him if he was ok and then, "Why are you here and how can I help you?" Once I opened a door to communication, he gave me the whole story. What I was getting from this intuitive and energetic conversation was that sometimes when we transition after a sudden or unexpected death, a spirit can get lost or confused. There are many sources of light and it is not always clear where we are supposed to go. This man's name is Anthony and he wasn't sure how he ended up where he was and nothing looked familiar to him, so he just wandered around trying to find his way. His accumulating depression was unnerving to the other spirits he encountered and they avoided him which increased his level of despair. Anthony found a great light in Jonathan and was hoping that the boy would lead him somewhere familiar, but Jonathan only wanted to run and hide from the overwhelming sadness that was following him.

Since I was able to communicate with Jonathan, Anthony thought it would be a good idea to follow me and see if I would be able to help. I can see where many people would easily confuse Anthony's energy with a being a dark or evil entity that was trying to terminate people's lives by talking them into suicide. I believe that energy is energy, the only difference is what we attach to that energy. His intention was to have me on the other side with him so he wouldn't feel so sad and lonely anymore. The big issue for me was that I'd have to die to help him cure his loneliness even though he was trying to make my transition as easy as possible. This is the basis for so many horror stories as they all want you to come over to the 'dark side'. From where I see it, it isn't as much a dark side at all, as it is just a side of sadness, loneliness, and depression.

I thanked Anthony for his sorrowful story and asked him if he had been in a relationship while alive? He said no. I tried again, "Do you have any siblings you would like to see and be reconnected with?" He said he had none. "How about your mother? Would you like to see her?" I asked. Anthony said, "No.

Absolutely not." Someone still has issues with his mother, but that's not why I'm here. "Ok. Your dad, then?" I asked as I was running out of options. Anthony's energy lit up and he said, "Yes. I would really like to see my father again!"

So I again sent Luke out to locate Anthony's father and bring him back here. For the very first time, there seemed to be a glimmer of hope around Anthony and maybe even an impression of a smile. He was actually very happy to finally find his father again and the reunion created a palpable feeling of joy in the room. I wished them both to continue on with love and light and made Anthony promise never to come into direct contact with another human again. It was too devastatingly painful. He agreed and as they both left, something wonderful happened.

I could breathe again. I turned my head from right to left without any pain or tension at all. I stood up and the intense back pain was gone instantly. What was even more evident was this feeling of elation. It felt like my heart was floating, my level of happiness was through the roof and my energy levels were not only back, but elevated. I felt tremendous. I had to sit down for a moment and try to understand everything I had just gone through and why.

We all have these wonderful spirit guides who are with us 24/7 and protect and guide us through our lives. Did mine suddenly develop a need to take a vacation and not tell me? Maybe this whole day had slipped through the crack and I was left to fend on my own. If I was at a point of jumping in front of a bus, I would like to think they would at least intervene and prevent that disaster from happening. As I was trying to understand why they didn't protect me from this depression, I began to get their messages along with an explanation.

They told me that they were not on vacation at all, but here with me the entire time. It was important for me to experience these events for myself, or I wouldn't believe just how powerful spiritual energies can be. They wanted to show me that we are greatly influenced by the energies around us and what kind of energies we attract.

Granted, I probably would not have believed or fully understood what severe depression was like unless I went through it myself. Remember, I am the eternal optimist, so what could I possibly know about the profound impact of depression? I went to school for engineering and can totally understand how energies can attract and repel but had no idea that spiritual energies could entice me to jump in front of a bus and commit suicide. I'd been through too many close calls and my near death experience to just end it all by stepping off a curb.

Reflecting back on the pain I experienced from Anthony, I assumed it was his way of getting my attention and creating an undesirable living situation and environment that would encourage me to join him on the other side. Why suffer through such intense pain and depression when an easy solution was right in front of me in the form of a friendly bus? After I had time to process all that had happened I realized Anthony was showing me how he died, with crushing spine and skull injuries and he was just sharing information with me and that's how it manifested. At the time I was just in too much pain to rationalize what was happening to me. I was even thinking of going to the emergency room at the hospital, but the doctors would not have found anything if this pain was projected. I knew the source. I just had to find out the why.

I've been working with clients for over 10 years now, helping them with everything from clearing clutter to increased energy and creative flow. Now I am dealing with their ghosts, spirits and dead relatives to help alleviate depression and thoughts of suicide and to create peace and understanding. My client's pain and depression would show immediate improvement during a session, but I had not learned how to protect myself and had to learn all of my lessons the hard way.

I started working with a new client who was in pain and had so many disturbing energies around her that I forgot to take care of myself after her session. I unintentionally took some of that energy home with me. Later that night I woke up suffering with a bad headache and back pain. After experiencing this a few times, I decided that I was done with all of it. I promised myself that this pain was not worth pursuing the work anymore. I was at a point where I just gave up and said I can't do any more clearings if each time these energies are going to jump on me and cause me pain.

It culminated to one night when I woke up extremely angry and yelling at whatever it was to get off me and get out of my house. I can tell you this approach does not work well at all. The last thing you want to do to a spirit that is lost, depressed, and seeking help, is to call it names, yell at it, and tell it to go away. Who wants a pissed off ghost after them? Once I learned how to reach out and create an open, loving channel with them, communication was easy. I was able to find out who they are, what they needed and could offer my help to get them connected to loved ones again.

One of the great things they have shown me is an outpouring of how they feel. This intense feeling of spiritual love and gratitude has none of the boundaries that we humans place on our emotions. I try to explain to people that it's like I'm under a waterfall of emotion and energy and information. It comes intensely and quickly until I have to remind them again that I am human and I can't handle the overwhelming quantities they are subjecting me to. Think of a time when you were most loved in your life. Multiply that feeling times 10. Multiply that again by 20. Now try to explain that emotion to another human using normal speech and words. That is one of my dilemmas. I wish you could feel what I feel.

What am I supposed to take away from all this? Everything they've shown me has always had a message or lesson attached. They say people hear things when they're ready to hear things. If other energies have the capacity to bond to our own electrical centers, our spine, shoulders, neck and head and the bonding causes pain and discomfort in those areas that could lead to more destructive vices like depression, addiction, and thoughts of suicide, what would happen to these conditions if the energies were separated? Could the negative emotions and associated thoughts of pain dissipate as quickly as mine did? Would it not be worth a try if no medications and no side effects are involved? Let's take a look and see.

Chapter 11

LET GO OF MY SHOULDER
Client Stories, Discoveries and
Spirit Relocation

As you interact with the people around you, an energy exchange is inevitable and you end up transporting some of these energies home with you. They can drain your personal energy causing fatigue, confusion, creative blocks, stress, anxiety, depression and even physical pain. Each time you enter your home, you proceed to dump all of this newly attached energy on top of the energy already stuck within your space, including your electronic devices and possessions. You thought all you wanted to do was just relax, regroup and put your feet up. We all hold our emotions in our bodies, musculature and in our possessions. All of these energetic connections to your space and your belongings can weigh you down physically, mentally and emotionally.

As I was clearing out old energies for my clients and detaching their connections to their possessions, I began asking them about the other energies in the room. I thought I was just being empathetic to my client's spirit guides and ghosts that were around them. These connections with their spirits were getting stronger and I could sense or "feel" information from them. I would have conversations with the entities in their home to see if they would be happier someplace else. My clients started calling me their "Energy Therapist" and then their own personal "Ghostbuster", although I don't really bust ghosts. I just find out where they are supposed to be, more like "Ghost Relocation Services".

I was self-taught when it came to dealing with spirit's connections to people and suffered the consequences, as with the devastating connection I shared with Anthony. I just assumed since the spirits were causing distress to my client, they had to leave. I chose to stop doing this work on several occasions because it became too physically painful when I could not shake them off of me.

At the time, I was unaware of how to properly communicate with these spirits. I would basically just tell them to get out and, to use the proverbial Poltergeist expression, "go into the light," which resulted in them getting even more confused and extremely annoyed with me. Each of us projects our own light and there are so many illuminated options in the spirit world that it only adds to their uncertainty.

They would just turn around and latch onto me, resulting in severe headaches, back pain, and confusion. After a few of these episodes, I began testing different approaches. I would offer an apology and ask them what they were looking for and why they were here. I learned to establish a connection with a loved one or family member who could escort them to where they were meant to be. I learned that "If something is done with love, you can never do it wrong!"

Clients are referred to me because they have very specific symptoms and I will know through a series of questions if I am able to help them. In most cases, they have experienced an intense change of mood and physical pain that comes on very quickly without any apparent reason. Doctors won't find anything wrong, X-rays will be normal and anti-depressants will only be effective temporarily. Pain medications will be prescribed and continued because the reason for the pain has not gone away which can lead to further addiction and depression. I ask my clients if they can they still feel what I call their "Authentic Voice". Your authentic voice is your inside or intuitive voice you were born with. Chances are none of us were born depressed, suicidal, anxious, worried or fearful. Once they can acknowledge their authentic voice, I ask them to differentiate that voice from the voice of depression and tell me where they feel it is coming from. I have them create distance from the voice of depression and continue to separate it away from themselves.

As my client is doing this, I begin to pick up some emotional energy from the spirit nearby. The spirits of children can be more of a roller coaster experience, depending on their mood. They enjoy playing with lights, electrical switches and even tossing things across the room. Once the connection is made, I can feel all the pain, loneliness, and sadness of the spirit which comes in large, overwhelming waves. My only vindication at this point is that this when the spirit is successfully reunited with a loved one, I also share the joy, release, and fulfillment they are experiencing. This feeling sometimes lasts for hours even after my client's session is over. That is my favorite part!

I will ask the spirit questions and try to establish whether the spirit is related to my client. Having either a family or love connection is of significant importance. Depending upon the point of contact, this connection usually results in back, neck and shoulder pain as well as intense headaches or migraines.

Our loved ones don't intend on inflicting us with pain but are just trying to get our attention by connecting to one or more of our electrical centers. After a time, these pains can lead to confusion, depression, medications, and addictions. The strongest connections we have are undeniably our love connections with family and loved ones and that is why I focus on reuniting them instead of sending spirits into the light.

Some spirits just want us to know they are nearby and are trying to help and comfort us, while others have a message that they need to share. They may want to tell a loved one that they are happy and doing fine where they are, or maybe a need to settle an unresolved issue or concern with someone. Other times they can be hopelessly lost and in need of a little help and guidance. Whatever their reason, this close proximity to humans can end up unintentionally causing us great pain and anxiety.

A spirit who is lost may have different intentions. They may be just hanging out with a client because they don't know they are dead yet. They are confused, depressed and have discovered a level of comfort with that person so they enjoy being with them. Unfortunately, this close proximity of their energy creates the same feeling of loneliness, depression, pain, and despair in my client and that energy needs to be redirected.

Afterwards, I have to keep in touch with my client. It's not like curing a cold or putting a Band-Aid over a scrape and then sending them on their way. I am talking about someone who has been enduring constant pain, possibly leading to addictions or thoughts of deep depression and suicide. I am not a doctor and I am not prescribing any medications with adverse side effects. I am simply having a conversation with an energy that may have severely harmful repercussions on my client.

I instruct my clients keep a journal and self-monitor themselves daily, preferably at the same time each day. I want them to write down how they are feeling at this moment not only physically, but also their hunger levels, abdominal tension, anxiety, body aches, breathing, heart palpitations, how they are interacting with others, and how they are feeling about getting their life back on track once again.

Depending on how long my client has been experiencing their symptoms, results can be immediate. As the energy shifts around them over the next few weeks, they can perceive incremental changes in mood and energy. As the stress and tensions leave, so do the associated headaches, shoulder, neck and back pain. They will also observe an increase in energy, mental clarity, focus and creativity along with a feeling of freedom, release, and joy. My clients also reported that they were able to sleep longer and deeper without interruption for the first time in years. The results speak for themselves. Here are some of their stories.

Paul

Paul is originally from North Buffalo, and I grew up in South Buffalo. I have known Paul and his family for over twenty years. Paul is deaf and so is the majority of his family, including his mother and father. Paul's father passed away several years ago leaving his wonderful mother, Joan, alone in the house with their dog Mickey. Paul takes his vacation time twice a year to go back home from Los Angeles and visit his mother. He just texted me from there and told me that the dog was acting strangely and he wanted to know what to do.

For the past few weeks, Mickey would sit in the middle of the living room floor, staring at the wall and start shaking. Paul was concerned, so he would pick the dog up and carry him into the next room where the shaking would immediately stop. Deaf people are more intuitively aware of their surroundings and pay more attention to body language. Paul and his mom both felt a presence in the house and saw the dog react to something being there. Paul watched the dog stare at someone pacing back and forth in the dining room when there was no one else in the room. When Paul released the dog, Mickey walked back into the living room, stared at the wall and began shaking again. Paul used sign language and started yelling at the spirit to get out of the house and not to come back, followed by a very cold feeling in the room.

Once he told me this story, I instantly knew what was going on. I told Paul not to yell at this spirit. You don't want to make him angry. Just be nice and ask him what he wants. Paul responded, "I can't hear what the ghost wants!" I told him I know that and I want you to use your intuition to see if you can feel anything. I already knew who was in the house, but I wanted him to find out for himself.

Paul's mom is 80 years old now and still does everything by herself, including taking care of an aging dog. There is a wonderful TV/video service that he uses in LA to talk directly to his mom on the TV and therefore, no interpreter is necessary. This way he can keep in touch with his mom in case she ever needs anything, even though he is still over 2,000 miles away. She and her husband were very close and it has been very hard on her living alone, especially through the cold Buffalo winters. I finally told Paul that the spirit in the house is his dad and he should talk to him and ask him how he is doing. He is there in the house because he is very worried about your mother and doesn't want to leave her alone. He is trying to help, so right now, I don't feel any need to relocate him. If Joan starts to have feelings of confusion or depression, then I will need to have her husband move on and join his family. We will continue to monitor her every day.

Marcy

A wonderful new client was referred to me when she was experiencing heart palpitations, anxiety, high blood pressure and depression. She felt that there was something strange in her apartment, but wasn't sure just what it was. When I began getting feelings of someone close to her that had a message for her, she mentioned it might be her uncle. I was getting a stronger emotional connection and asked her about her husband.

This sweet woman told me she survived a 30-year abusive relationship with her husband, Andy, who eventually committed suicide. As she was talking I started getting heart palpitations myself and it felt like Andy had reached inside my chest and squeezed my heart. She said she didn't think it was Andy because they don't have anything to say to each other and their relationship was finished a long time ago. I told her he's holding onto your heart because he's sorry and needs to apologize for his terrible behavior when you were together. He's desperately hoping you find it in your heart to forgive him. She said she would and then I helped Andy reunite with his mom who had also transitioned, so he could move on. Marcy monitored her energetic improvements over the next few weeks as her blood pressure and heart issues lessened.

A few weeks later, while I was having my morning coffee, I noticed I was getting these annoying heart palpitations. I stopped taking all my vitamins, amino acids and even stopped having coffee in the morning to see if that would help. This went on for a few days and I started to get concerned, thinking I might need to start doing cardio in the mornings or make an appointment to see my doctor. One night before bed, I did an energy check on myself to see if anyone else was hanging around me.

I suddenly remembered my new client with the heart palpitations that I did the clearing for about 2 weeks ago. I reconnected Andy to his mother, so I asked Andy why he was back and if there was anything I could help him with. He said he wasn't ready to go with his mother yet, and I was the last person he spoke to, so he thought he'd come back and hang out with me. Apparently, Andy was unaware he had actually died in his suicide attempt!

So, now am I not only redirecting spirits, I have to be the bearer of bad news and also tell them when they are DEAD! He did not take the news well and seemed very upset. To comfort him, I brought in both his mom and dad along with his grandmother and grandfather to happily take him to join the rest of his spiritual family.

I knew this connection was the right one now because as soon as they all left, I became overwhelmed with Andy's sadness and confusion about dying along with the joy and love he had for his family. I started crying heavily under the intensity of all the emotion. I contacted my client to tell her sometimes these spirit connections are not as clean and easy as they seem. I explained what happened the second time around and hopefully now he's happy wherever he is now.

Douglas

I was referred to a client in Florida who had unusual electrical and plumbing failures constantly in his home. My client also was suffering from severe back pain after multiple surgeries. He told me he could feel there was an interfering, denser energy but did not know what was happening or why. The upsets were happening for the past 10 years that he and his partner had lived in the house.

I was aware of a male energy that had an emotional connection to Doug, so I asked him about his father. Doug told me he never had a good relationship with his father. His dad was very controlling and had been dead for about 10 years. It was very clear to me at that point what was going on.

I asked Doug if his father was an electrician and he sounded very surprised. "Yes, he was. How did you know that?" he asked me. I began filling him in on all the information I was receiving from his dad. "Your dad loves you very much and has been doing everything he possibly could over the past ten years to get your attention," I told him. "He has been actually holding onto your lower back to let you know how much he loves you and needs to apologize for not being there for you. Maybe he was also doing that to try to continue controlling you. When that didn't work, he started shorting out all of the electrical renovations you've been doing on your home. Does any of this make sense to you?" I asked him. He said it made enormous sense.

I connected his dad back with his family so Doug could continue living his life without anyone else around trying to control him and tell him what to do. It was like a rock was lifted off his shoulders. His therapist was sitting in on our session and when Doug got up to go to the bathroom, the therapist told me she has never seen Doug stand up straight like did just now in all the years she has known him. The therapist could also feel the shift in the house and its energy and immediately following the redirection of the spirit, Doug said he could feel his shoulders and legs release. It was truly a profound healing experience for my client and the spirits involved.

Cynthia

I was talking to a yoga instructor at my gym while she was rubbing her shoulder. I asked what was wrong and she showed me where her pain was. It started up behind her ear, down her neck, and into her shoulder. I asked her how long this man has been with her. Cynthia is aware of the work I do, so she wasn't totally surprised by my question, it was just something she hadn't thought of before.

She told me she had seen the spirit of a man twice inside her apartment in the last week. She asked me to help her and since we were alone inside the gym studio, I continued. I asked the man why he was holding onto to Cynthia's shoulder and he said he really liked her energy. I explained to him the hazards to coming in contact with a human and how much pain it causes. He apologized and said he was only trying to help. I asked him if there was anyone special that he would he like to reconnect with and he told me that he lost a daughter and would love to see her again. Once they were reunited, he was delighted and thrilled to join her and thanked me as they left. I told Cynthia to sleep on it and we'd talk in the morning.

The next day Cynthia came running up to me at the gym while I was talking to two other clients of mine. She said this was the first day in over a full year that she did not experience any pain in her neck and shoulder. She had gone to chiropractors, doctors, acupuncturists, and nutritionists, with no relief. She was so grateful that she asked me to perform a clearing on her home.

Ken

Ken said that he was not the only person who felt something strange every time he entered his apartment. He had just ended a long relationship and wanted me to clear out the old energy and do an exorcism on whatever sort of entity was inside his place. I told Ken that I do not just get rid of entities and I never force them to leave. That only makes them angry and upset with me. I explained that I would have a conversation with whatever was there and see how I would be able to help. Ken agreed and we set up an appointment for one night after he finished work.

I knew there was something in his apartment as soon as I arrived, but I wanted to concentrate on clearing the energy first, then I would deal with the entity. I have a procedure I use for clearing where I go through the entire house removing all the old, stuck energy. I then use the energy of the owner to fill the space, providing clarity and creative flow. Afterwards, we sat down to concentrate on who was in the apartment.

Usually, I sense spirits at their normal height of around seven feet tall. As we sat at the dining room table, I sensed someone quite small. It was a short, older woman with white hair, glasses and a strong emotional connection to Ken. I asked Ken if any of this sounds familiar and if her name started with an "A". "Agnes!" he shouted. "That's my grandmother!" he confirmed. He also said they weren't very close as she was more involved with the rest of the family. I assured him that is why she is here. She wants to him to know that she was extremely sorry for their lack of connection over the years, and she wanted him to know that she is here for him now if he ever needs anything.

Ken was happy that I not only regenerated his living space but was able to re-connect him with his grandmother; not an evil entity at all. He seemed very grateful and comforted to know she is still around and looking out for him.

John

John moved into a new apartment in Fort Lauderdale and even after two months, was not able to sleep. He told me that he felt something heavy in his space and whatever this was, it wanted a lot of attention to the point of shaking his bed in the middle of the night.

I explained to John that a ghost is just a spirit that somehow got stuck. I asked him if there were any drugs or alcohol in the apartment that might be causing some lower frequency entities to come in. He assured me that there were none, but possibly something from the apartment next door. I could feel the spirit of a young, Latino boy in the bathroom by the wall of the shower. John told me that was the adjoining wall to the apartment next door where all the partying was going on.

This boy's name was George or Jorge, and he had some connection to what was happening next door but kept coming over here hoping John would help him. That's why he was shaking the bed every night. Possibly young Jorge had died of a drug overdose and that would explain his connection to the adjacent apartment.

I told Jorge this could not be a fun place to hang out and asked if he had any family members he'd like to see. He said there was none. "Not even your grandmother of grandfather?" I asked. He still said no. "Well, maybe my aunt," he confessed. I quickly connected Jorge with his aunt before he changed his mind and I could feel Jorge was very happy to see her again. His aunt grabbed his arm to take him away, but

Jorge refused to leave. I told Jorge he needed to go with his aunt and join the rest of his family instead of hanging out in a bathroom.

I asked his aunt who could help her and she told me her husband would help. We were able to find Jorge's uncle and once they were positioned on each side of him, he relented and agreed to go. I told him he would be in a much better place, and I sent them along with love and light. I texted John that Jorge had left with his aunt and uncle and wouldn't be back to shake your bed any longer. John thanked me and has been having relaxed nights of much-needed sleep ever since.

Tim

For several months Tim had dark thoughts, depression, and a constant nagging that he just wasn't himself, even having thoughts of suicide. He tried botanicas, home cleansings, positive affirmations, and read almost every book on ghosts and possessions he could get his hands on, but he felt there was no one he could talk to about this. Tim was referred to me through a hypnotherapist friend of mine and I immediately sensed a presence around him, confirming my suspicions. I reminded him that spirits of the dead can affect the living but should not to be feared, as they're in as much pain as they inflict upon us. I knew that love and empathy for the lost spirit were essential as it needed attention and reunion with a loved one to move on.

Tim picked up a ghost named Henry from the old, historic apartment building he was managing in Hollywood. These old, grand buildings hold lots of memories for spirits that don't want to move on. When they feel comfortable with someone or maybe just attracted to their light, they begin to follow that person. All of the spirit's emotions of sadness, loss, confusion, and depression will transfer to the person unintentionally. That is why Tim's life until recently, was happy and full of the joy he received from his wife, two kids, and his work.

He woke up one morning feeling depressed and had no idea why. Nothing had changed and his life was the same as it was the day before, but now his joy was replaced with daily thoughts and plans of suicide. These transfers of emotion can happen that quickly, leaving the person trying to analyze themselves on a daily basis in an attempt to understand why their life had changed so drastically.

I don't find these spirits to be malevolent or evil, just terribly lost, confused, and depressed. If they see a compassionate human with great light surrounding them, they innocently would like us to join them to keep them company. That is where the deep thoughts and justification for suicide come in.

They make it seem very clear and easy to do, but at such a great cost to us. I believe that we are all here to learn something and suicide is like taking an illegal shortcut with severe ramifications on the other side.

So, Henry seemed like a very kind ghost and enjoyed being around Tim. I explained to Henry that he is causing Tim great pain and discomfort by just being near him, so need to find him a more suitable situation. I began asking him if he had any siblings he would like to see again. He told me no. I asked him if he was married and he told me he was. His wife's name was Roselyn. I instantly sent my guide Luke out to find Roselyn and bring her back to Henry. I could feel them both side by side once she was brought in, but strangely, I felt nothing more.

Usually, I get an enormous rush of energy, information, and emotion. I was feeling nothing, so I asked Henry if something was wrong. Henry tells me that he didn't particularly care to see his wife again. That was my mistake for not asking the proper question. I then asked Henry who he'd like to see right now and he told me his mother. He'd really love to see his mother. Luke was sent off yet again to locate Henry's mother and as soon as she arrived, I was so overwhelmed with emotion the only way I could handle it all was to burst out crying uncontrollably. It was not a sad feeling, just a rush of so many feelings of happiness and joy that as a human it is difficult to process. I said hello to Henry's mother and asked her to please take both Henry and Roselyn to wherever they need to be to join the rest of their family members. I instructed Henry not to come into direct contact with humans again because of the consequences. He agreed and I sent them all on with love and light.

What happened next was really wonderful. For the next two hours, I continued getting residual emotions of freedom, love, and joy from Henry and didn't know what to do with so much happiness. Now if I could just bottle this emotional energy and distribute it, that would be tremendous!

I texted Tim when I was done and told him to monitor himself in his journal at least once a day for the next few weeks to track his improvement. He responded that he instantly felt more at peace, balanced, and grounded and by morning woke with a new and refreshed outlook on life. The feelings of depression and suicide were gone, without any medical or pharmaceutical side effects. He thanked me for reinforcing the belief that life is more than meets the eye. Life is about the journey of our souls.

Three weeks later Tim invited me in to see the old apartment building he helps manage. Located in the historic area near Hollywood and Vine, this 10-story building was constructed in 1924 and was home to silent film star Clara Bow. Over the years the building has endured a variety of renovations that has left the building in an odd blend of old grandeur and new drywall.

Most of the tenants here are seniors and the building is filled with spirits that are upset about the neglect of their favorite property. He escorted me to the back storage room where he said he wanted to show me something. I didn't see anything unusual, but I felt something like I had never felt before! We were suddenly surrounded by spirit energy so thick, it was as if we both had an invisible electric curtain or blanket over us, fully covering our skin. It was gentle but definitely electrical and tingled in a really delightful way. I had a slight taste of aluminum on my tongue as I thanked the spirits in the room for sharing that wonderful feeling with us. I turned to Tim and said I think we just experienced our first spiritual group hug!

As Tim was showing me around this amazing property, we ended the tour in the gardens behind the building. This small oasis has a collection of palm trees, plants, flowers and a gazebo. I stopped short by a tall palm tree and once again felt every hair from my toes to the top of my ears stand on end. I grabbed Tim's arm and asked him if he felt that. He said he did and knew what it was from. He instructed me to look up at the top of the building. Just six months earlier, one of the caretakers of the building had jumped from the ten-story roof to his death. He landed on the stone covered ground beneath my feet. Two months later, a tenant followed the same path, landing in the exact same place.

I felt the sadness of the spirits in the building and how upset they were. These energies and emotions can easily be transferred to anyone in the building and unfortunately for the receiving human, they won't be able to understand where these feelings of depression and sadness are coming from. They will feel as if there is something wrong with them. The spirits only want to share their unhappiness and have someone acknowledge them and what they are going through.

As we walked around to the front of the building, I was feeling a sense of joy from inside the old structure because they felt that someone finally is paying attention to them and feeling their frustration. Before I left, I actually yelled out to them saying it was nice meeting you all, letting them know if anyone needed to be relocated to their families, to please let me know. I asked nicely that none of them follow me home because I will come back to visit them whenever I'm in the neighborhood. I told them not to get too close to the humans in the building because I didn't want any more tenants leaping off the top floor. As I drove away, it felt like a happy group of ghosts finally had something pleasant to talk about.

Chapter 12

GHOST MESSAGES
What I have learned

How do you know if you have ghosts around you?

Pay attention to the signs around you, especially to the songs you hear in your head. Sometimes it will sound like a song you are hearing in another room, but it is actually a reignited memory telling you that someone is around and trying to get your attention. A special song might suddenly be on the radio in the car, or again in the grocery store and then again in a restaurant. They will keep playing their favorite song until you start to acknowledge that you are hearing it. Try and recall the memory of the song and who you shared the memory with. Don't be afraid to say hello to who you feel might be there with you and ask them how they are doing.

Watch for visual signs that repeat or show up at an unexpected moment. A client of mine was a caretaker for her mother for many years. Her nephews had a nickname for their grandmother. They called their mother, "Little Mommy" and their grandmother "Big Mommy", or "Biggie".

A month after my client's mother died, she was driving her nephews home and they were saying how much they missed "Biggie". At the very next stoplight, she happened to glance down at the license plate of the car in front of her and on the plate was the word, "Biggie". She took that as a wonderful sign that her mom was still present and looking out for the nephews, and her as well.

We respond to our spiritual connections in various ways. You might suddenly receive a strong intuitive feeling or experience the onset of goose bumps along the back of your arms and the hair on the back of your neck may begin to stand on end. Although this concept was borrowed in most horror movies whenever a ghost was around, this is an electrical response to your connection. Now you have to just re-associate it with the spirit of a loved one or someone you were close to.

My brother deals with missing things in his house all the time. These are usually small items that are always kept in the same place until they disappear like your keys, wallet, and glasses. Pay attention intuitively and not with your eyes or your ears to see which spirits might be playing these games with you. Consider what you are feeling at the moment and make an attempt to communicate. You could be very surprised by the result.

Spirits love to play with electrical devices such as televisions, lights and light switches, doorbells, breakers, etc. If that doesn't work to get your attention, they may start throwing things. After having my first conversation with my new clients in Hollywood, I knew there was the spirit of a little girl in their house, along with several other spirits and energies on the property. The night before I was to meet my new clients, she decided to get my attention by throwing my gym bag across the bedroom and onto the floor at 5 am, and on a very warm summer night, she turned on the heater in my apartment. Her message to me was that she liked where she was very much and didn't want to be relocated. Message delivered!

Another very important occurrence to observe are any sudden unexplained body aches, pain or depression. The body aches will again be centered around your electrical centers like your back, spine, shoulders, neck, and head. That means that someone is around you and you need to pay attention. They don't mean to cause you pain, but they really want you to know they are there. If you can't hear their message, then you need to find someone who can. Once the message is conveyed, they have the freedom to move on. Don't suffer needlessly.

Spirits are not dead

Spirits tell me they don't like being referred to as 'dead'. They are not dead in their eyes. They see everything we see and more. 'Spirit energy' is a much better reference than being 'dead'. Maybe their messages aren't so obvious to us, but if you pay attention and trust your intuition, you will begin to notice things. Spirits are all at different levels of learning, just as we are. As our guides help us through life, they are also learning and growing from us at the same time.

We do have a strong life-long connection with our spirit guides and they are accessible anytime we need them. I have three guides. Luke is the youngest and is my 'go-to' guide whenever I need him to connect and find someone for me. Noah is my guide for strength. He usually puts his hand on my head so I know he's there. Abe is my older guide who tries to keep me grounded in reality. He is usually quiet but does kick me in the butt now and then to help keep me focused. Our guides are always with us and when we think they're not here helping us, it is usually because they don't want to interfere with a lesson we are about to learn. We are not being ignored.

Besides our guides, there are all of our friends and relatives who have transitioned over and are all busy doing the things they need to do. We all have connections with anyone who has passed on and they are here whenever we need them. Instead of always asking them for help and guidance, they do appreciate it when you take the time and ask them how they are doing, if they need anything, and then show them a little gratitude for all they've done.

Although it is wonderful for them to hang out with us, I find that when we get too close to them and ask too many questions, they can quickly shut the door on us. Our job here is to learn and appreciate life, moment to moment, knowing where we have been and looking forward to where we are going. They don't want us to learn too much about the rest of the universe because it creates a distraction from what we should be doing here on earth and the lessons we need to learn. Everything will be clearer once we transition.

The difference between a ghost and a spirit

Spirits are around us all the time, along with our spirit guides. We all have them and whether you are aware of them or not, they are here. I would go to a party crowded with people and not only would I have to deal with all the conversations happening with everyone present, then there were all of the energetic conversations happening with everyone's guides and spirits. It would get overwhelming and the interesting message I would get from them is that people don't utilize them enough.

There is an even deeper thought that we chose our spirit guides to help us on our learning path here on earth even before we were born. This would mean that we were also involved in choosing our parents, family, and conditions for this life to learn the valuable lessons we were meant to learn. Whatever the intention was, they are here for us now and there should be no reason why we wouldn't want to include them in our daily lives. They help me all the time with anything from life changing decisions, finding the perfect parking space, to even writing this book.

Lost spirits are ones I refer to as ghosts and they can potentially have harmful effects on us. Most of the near-death experiences have the same scenario. They can see themselves floating above their body and traveling into a tunnel of light. This tunnel is filled with all of their family waiting to greet them and inform them that it was not their time yet, so they were instructed to return to their bodies and continue with their life. This could be termed a "Return To Sender" tunnel. If someone dies suddenly and they transition too quickly, they say there was no tunnel. Sometimes they hang around us because they don't know they are dead yet. Other times if a loved one dies they may hang around waiting for some completion of their own unresolved issues.

The longer they remain lost, the more confused and depressed they get. When they hang around us, we feel and connect with their energy causing us to be upset and miserable also. When ghosts get lost, the strongest connection they will have is to family and loved ones, not someone else's light. My work has been to connect these lost ghosts back to their families and those they love.

Be careful what you watch

One of the big messages I get is how much we are susceptible to the energies around us. If our brain functions as a computer and accepts the information it is given, then why are we watching so much of the disturbing programming on television today? Just 20 years ago television viewing was so much different. We never had so much violence, sex, theft, murder, and crime on at our prime time TV watching. If we are at home and relaxed and passively watching all this, does that it become the new normal for living today? If it is ok to pick up a gun on TV and shoot someone, is it, therefore, ok to pick up a gun at home and take it school?

When the news gets too depressing, I have to turn it off. If the show I am watching is about demons, vampires or possessions, I have to turn it off. Pay attention to the energy in your home. They tell us we should not be relaxing to violence. If you want to relax, listen to music, read a book or find something enjoyable to watch that lowers your blood pressure. We are all empathetic to a point where this all has to start affecting us at a very deep level.

How much are we being programmed by our viewing? As we are watching all of our favorite cop shows and solving murder mysteries, is our mind really capable of turning off the commercials or are we subliminally programming ourselves to all the pharmaceutical ads? Everything from shingles, cancer, diabetes, fibromyalgia, allergies, migraines, psoriasis, flu and colds, ulcers, restless leg syndrome, blood pressure, ulcerative colitis, copd, colon cancer, toenail fungus, heart problems, sensitive teeth and gums, back pain, dry eyes, and so on. You name it and there's a cure for it in a television commercial, along with an unusually long list of potential side effects. Anyone watching all this from outside the US might think, "Those poor Americans have SO many diseases, no wonder their medical insurance rates are so high!"

Our best natural immune boosters

Ginger and garlic. Listen to your body and when you start to feel heavy, tired and achy, it's time for a boost. Wash and cut a sugar cube sized chunk of fresh ginger root and chew it. The flavor is spicy and intense, so you can start with a smaller piece. Suck the juices out and throw the pulp away and follow with a large glass of water. Do this at least twice a day.

My other good tip is fresh garlic. I like to use a nice soup base like lentil, vegetable or chicken noodle and at the last minute, slice 6 to 8 cloves of garlic into the soup. You don't want to overcook the garlic because you can lose some of the powerful effects of the garlic. Both ginger and garlic are great immune boosters, unless you are allergic or just cannot tolerate the taste. You don't need a prescription and there is no long list of side effects.

My grandmother gave me some great advice (years after she passed away). We go to bed when we are sick and wake up feeling worse. We breathe our germs into our pillow each night then go about our day taking care of ourselves as best we can. If we go back to bed without changing our pillowcase, we will re-infect ourselves with the germs from the night before. Just change your pillowcase before going to sleep, or turn your pillow over so you don't re-infect yourself. This is so simple and effective that it's easy to forget. You might have to stick a post-it note on your pillow in the morning as a reminder.

I also have a great "Bath Soup" that will remove toxins from your body, allow you to get an amazing night of deep sleep and wake up feeling great. Toss 3 big handfuls of Epsom salt, 3 handfuls of baking soda, a 3-second pour of hydrogen peroxide, a few dashes of eucalyptus oil or Tea Tree oil and even 5 or 6 slices of ginger into a hot tub and then soak for 20 minutes.

Afterwards, remove the ginger so you do not clog your drain and open the plug in the tub. Watch and feel the water drain around you. Be aware of the salts pulling toxins and germs from your body, into the water, and down the drain. Along with it, let go of any negative thoughts, emotions or energies and feel them leaving you as you become even more relaxed in the tub. Dry off and pour yourself into bed for an amazingly deep sleep (on your fresh pillow case!)

Here is another great and easy thing I like to do after I've been on a plane or in a public place with other people that may be sneezing or coughing. Our mouths can handle germs because of our saliva. Our eyes, nose, and ears are open portals for germs to enter. Of course, wash your hands and face, but here's another great prevention. Take a cotton swab and dip it into hydrogen peroxide and wipe the inside of both nostrils. Take another swab with hydrogen peroxide and gently wipe your outer ear canal. This will kill any germs that are even thinking about entering your body.

These remedies are so simple, easy to do and at very little cost but I find that even with my best clients, we as Americans are so programmed to going to our doctors and getting Z-packs, antibiotics, cough and cold remedies, and antihistamines that dry us up and interfere with my number one treatment suggestion of keeping your body flowing. Also, remember to shop the perimeters of the grocery store. That is where all the fresh food products are. Try these first and see the results for yourself. My guides are rarely wrong.

Animals see things we don't

• I think everyone has an animal story about their favorite pet reacting to something that no one else can see. The perfect example was when I was staying with a friend in Hollywood who had the cutest little Boston terrier. I was doing my father's favorite tradition around the holidays, handwriting Christmas cards while watching the inevitable annual holiday animated TV shows.

The little terrier walks in and sits down a few feet in front of the table I was working on and looks up at me. She is very affectionate and rarely barks so I was very surprised at her next reaction. I was just sitting there thinking about my dad who didn't have to do this seasonal task anymore and wondering if he missed it when the little dog's head turns a bit and focuses on the blank wall behind me.

She starts barking like crazy while staring at this blank spot. There is nothing there on the wall and she's not jumping or running around, but just sitting there barking. I finally looked over my left shoulder and said to the wall, "Dad, it's always great to see you, but you're scaring the dog!" As soon as I said that, she immediately stopped barking, walked over to her bed and laid down. Thanks for popping in to say hello, Dad!

- I just moved into my new apartment downtown and the first thing I always do is clear the energy out of a new space. It's not either good energy or bad energy, but I like it to be my own. I just finished my clearing and as I was leaving my new place my neighbor, Larena, had stopped by to say hello with her little miniature Doberman. The dog looks up at me with those great big eyes, turns to look at my door, then faces the door and sits.

As we are talking, someone walks off the elevator and as they are walking past us, the dog goes into attack mode, barking at the poor person just trying to sneak by. As soon as they pass, the dog once again faces the door, looks at the door about 3/4 of the way up and sits.

As Larena decides to go back to her place and pulls on the dog's leash, the dog does not budge. No barking. No sniffing around the door. Just sits. She asked me what I had done inside that might be catching all of the dog's attention and I told her I had just cleared the energy in my space. I didn't even have any food in there yet. Another person tries to walk by and the dog goes crazy again, barking and jumping around. And then he sits again. We decided that this dog would officially be Larena's energy guide dog from now on.

• I was on my way to a client's home in Beverly Hills and parked about a block away. As I was walking down the street, I could see two older women walking slowly toward me with a small dog on a leash. The little dog looked as though he was leading them down the street.

As they got closer, I could see it looked like a terrier mix, with great big eyes. I noticed as we locked eyes, his tail started wagging and I thought he was just happy to receive some attention from a stranger.

Once he was in range, I knelt down and he came over to me with tongue extended, ready for licking, and overly happy to see me. The two women stopped and stared and asked me if I knew their dog. I told them that this was actually our first meeting and asked if he was always this friendly. They both said no, he wasn't and doesn't even greet them like this when they arrive home after being gone all day. They had never seen him react that way. I told them they had a very sweet dog and were very lucky owners, gave the pooch another hug and went on my way feeling great after a nice human and dog bonding!

Stop and notice where you are

I participated in the clinical trials for jet lag and while at the University of Surrey, just outside of London, the doctors governing the trials would give us questionnaires every 3 hours to see how we were doing. The fascinating thing was that my answers were not consistent. My mood would change quickly because I was either tired or hungry or both. My initial thought was that there would be no change during the day and all my reports would be the same. The result was quite the opposite. My mood would change from relaxed to stressed to anxious to angry very quickly.

The one important lesson here is that I want you to take a moment every day to just stop what you're doing, take a deep breath and ask yourself how you are feeling right now. Does anything hurt? Is anything bothering you? Do you have a roof over your head right now? Is there food in the refrigerator? Do you have clothes to wear? Have your bills been paid for the month? Do you have a car? A family? A relationship? Chances are that right now, everything is fine. This helps us to keep grounded and keep us present. If we are present, there is no fear. Fear is an emotion of the future, a 'what if' scenario. Right here, right now everything should be fine.

Stop trying to control everything. You chose this life and this existence to learn something. Let it unfold before you. Just observe it, don't force it. Relax and be grateful. Your lesson in this life is not to see how much stress you can handle!

Ask for help

Why is it so much easier to tell someone else what to do, when we find it so difficult to make decisions for ourselves? Sometimes things are actually too close to us for us to see clearly. It's hard to heal ourselves when we always have a different perspective of who we are. Healers say that we see ourselves upside down and backward! That's why we seek others for advice and guidance. You can't really give yourself a massage. Doctors can't operate on themselves and lawyers don't defend themselves. Let other people help. We always feel that we don't want to burden our friends and family with our difficult situations, but really, that's what they are here for! I always say, it never hurts to ask anyone for anything. The worst thing that will happen is that they say no!

A prayer is a just conversation to our guides who are watching out for us. Let your guides help. What they tell me is to request an "MBO"; Most Benevolent Outcome. This way your request is not just for your own good but also helps others in the wake. When trying to make a decision about which way something might need to go, just before bed I 'toss' the decision-making problem up to my guides, request the most benevolent outcome for all concerned and surrender! And don't forget to say, "Thank you!".

They know more than we do. They're not that busy. They don't sleep and they're here to help us, so let them help! Remember, we are all here to learn something and that lesson can be painful. We experience growth through pain, so keep on growing!

Chapter 13

STATISTICS
For Suicide, Pain and Depression

Suicide:

According to Wikipedia, an estimated one million people worldwide take their lives by suicide every year. Suicide ranks among the three leading causes of death in the world among those 15-44 and suicide attempts are up to 20 times more frequent than completed suicides. In the US, males are four times more likely to die by suicide than females, although more women than men report suicide attempts.

Over 44,000 people die by suicide each year in the US, which means that on the average there are 121 suicides per day, or one every 13 minutes, imposing a cost of $51 billion to the US annually. The highest rate of suicide is in middle age white males and military veterans have double the suicide rate of non-veterans.

Pharmaceuticals:

According to CBS News, researchers found that nearly 70 - 80 percent of Americans are on at least one prescription drug, and more than half receive at least two prescriptions. Twenty percent of US patients were also found to be on five or more prescription medications. Dr. St. Sauver stated in a Mayo Clinic press release, "Often when people talk about health conditions, they're talking about chronic conditions such as heart disease of diabetes. However, the second most common prescription was for antidepressants. That suggests mental health is a huge issue and is something we should focus on. The third most common drugs were opioids, which is a bit concerning considering their addicting nature."

Melody Petersen, author of "Our Daily Meds", presents an in-depth look at the pharmaceutical companies that have taken the reins of our faltering health care system by cleverly hawking every kind of drug imaginable. Melody wrote that 100,000 Americans die each year from prescriptions drugs, that's 270 per day or twice as many who are killed in car accidents each day.

Gender Identification:
There have been so many studies as to the cause of confusion in sexual orientation and identity. Socialization and environmental factors, biological factors of genes and hormone levels, genetic makeup and even brain structure have been a consideration in gender roles.

Depression:

Globally, more than 300 million people of all ages suffer from depression. Depression is different from usual mood fluctuations and short-lived emotional responses to challenges in everyday life. Many people with depression also suffer from anxiety symptoms, disturbed sleep, and appetite and may have feelings of guilt or low self-worth, poor concentration and even medically unexplained symptoms.

The US government seeks to prevent suicides through a plan consisting of eleven goals aimed at preventing suicides. What if all of the prescribed treatments, therapies and medications fail to work? What causes us to become so depressed and suicidal? Let's take a look at where all this depression is coming from.

I recently had a conversation with one of the US Government Funded Therapists at UCLA for soldiers returning from Afghanistan. I wanted to see how open they would be to alternative forms of therapy. He mentioned that through their research observing structural brain changes during meditation, they now incorporated meditation into their therapy sessions. That already is a huge step. These boys showed no sign of being depressed and suicidal when they went to Afghanistan but came home hearing a voice of depression and sadness that wasn't their own and the assigned therapies and treatments showed them no improvement, outside of meditation.

Instead of issuing medications, I would encourage the opportunity to investigate, through a simple process of a conversation, to see where this voice of depression and pain is located. I am certain the voice would not be their authentic voice. A war zone is filled with suddenly transitioning energies that are looking for direction. It is easy to see how some get lost and attract to our soldiers on their way home. Most of these spirits probably have no idea they're even dead yet. It would be amazing to observe that if by just removing these energies from around them, their levels of anxiety would not only diminish but disappear entirely, without any drugs or medications.

Most of my clients have already done the normal routine of trying to cure their depression. Doctors, therapies, medications, and treatments can all be beneficial, but when none of these remedies work, it's time to take a look at the energies surrounding them. I ask my clients a few questions about their symptoms to see when and how their symptoms began. The type of depression I'm looking for will come on very quickly and without any warning or reason. This level of depression is devastating and creates confusion and loneliness in my client and can be accompanied by physical pain as well as thoughts of suicide. As they continue to explain their situation to me, I will begin to feel if something is there with them. It usually hits me like a wave of the same emotion my client is experiencing.

I will attempt to get a name from the spirit and a brief story of what happened to them and how they ended up where they are, which will explain the intense emotion they are projecting. The spirit is usually pleased that someone is paying attention to them, showing them concern, and wanting to communicate. They have been lost and confused for an undetermined amount of time and having someone discover them, creates a hint of joy in their cloud of desperation.

I had a client that said he was born with depression and when I asked him if he felt it was his own authentic voice, he told me no. He said his grandmother was always depressed and he must have inherited from her. Could depression be inherited? I don't believe so.

I made him aware that it was his grandmother's spirit and energy hanging around him that was making him depressed. The important point is, if depression is all you've ever known, then when depression leaves are you able to handle feeling normal again? Some people feel a need to hang onto their stress, anxiety, pain, and depression because it has always been there and is comfortable for them.

Once I was able to distance his grandmother from him, he began to feel a shift in his own energy and can now choose for himself how he should feel.

Pharmaceuticals are easily distributed for any pain in your neck, shoulders, back, and head. Nothing the doctors, chiropractors, acupuncturists or massage therapists did had any beneficial results, and nothing showed up in X-rays. The medications themselves can lead to loneliness, confusion, depression and even addiction because none of the therapies, hypnosis treatments or detoxing methods worked. The contact points for this type of pain are usually from a spirit energy that we are familiar with and is just trying to get our attention. Their intention is out of love, but they are unaware that they are the cause of our pain.

Let's take a look at sexual identification. I find it fascinating that with all our technology today the doctors and scientists are not able to precisely discern the cause of confusion with sexual identity. The formation of gender identity in children is said to begin as early as 18 months and firmly formed by the age of three. They tend to choose activities and toys that are considered appropriate for their gender.

After age three, core gender identity is extremely difficult to change and attempts to reassign it result in gender dysphoria. If a female spirit in the hospital makes a connection to a new born baby boy, he is already being influenced by having a female energy surrounding him, making him think he is female. The same identity issue would hold in reverse if a baby girl was surrounded by the spirit of a boy and taking on that energy. I think it might be an excellent idea before anyone decides to go under a knife for a permanent sex change, to have a conversation about just where the voice of this other identity is coming from. It would make sense that original sex hormones would return and be functioning as they should with no need for any sexual identity transitions and confusion.

There are many of these spirit release conversations happening throughout England now. They say that the history of this work goes back to biblical times and has been around for centuries with great success. There is so much for all of us to learn about clearing these energies away and out of our daily lives. If this spirit relocation process continues to be such a great success, then the possibilities are limitless.

The world is changing quickly, along with our thoughts and views of spirituality. As the world's population increases, so do the number of spirits around us. Years ago, it may have been special to visit a haunted place and feel a presence. Today, I rarely find just one spirit in a house. They are usually in groups. When I visited the old Hollywood Plaza and toured the basement I waved my arm in front of me and must have passed through 8 or 10 spirits crowded around us. They really are everywhere and we must start becoming aware of their presence.

The spirits around us are intensely emotional beings and their energies can very easily assimilate into our own energies, feelings, and emotions. They aren't just Ghost Stories anymore, but part of our daily existence here. How wonderful it would be to have communication, assistance, cooperation, and awareness of all of the energies around us!

THANK YOU!

Thank you so much for sharing this journey with me. If we truly are here on this planet to learn our life lessons and to help others, then I hope everything I have learned can be put to good use.

The results I've had working with my clients have been tremendous and it warms my heart I may have made a difference in someone's life who was suffering.

For more information you can check out my website, send me an email or call the office for an appointment. Thank you for being part of my life.

Rick Wagner
myhauntedreality.com
myhauntedreality@gmail.com